Amazing Jewish Heroes
down through the Ages

Cover photograph of David Ben-Gurion: Georgios Kollidas/iStock/Thinstock
Cover photograph of Theodor Herzl: Photos.com/Photos.com/Thinkstock
Cover photograph of Zeev Jabotinsky: Jabotinsky Institute in Israel.
www.jabotinsky.org

Cover Design: Forever Studios
Typesetting: Ben Herskowitz
ISBN: 978-965-229-881-2

1 3 5 7 9 8 6 4 2

Gefen Publishing House Ltd.   Gefen Books
6 Hatzvi Street   140 Fieldcrest Ave.
Jerusalem 94386, Israel   Edison NJ, 08837
972-2-538-0247   516-593-1234
orders@gefenpublishing.com   orders@gefenpublishing.com

www.gefenpublishing.com

Printed in Israel

Library of Congress Cataloging-in-Publication Data

Names: Goldberg, David Richard, author.
Title: Amazing Jewish heroes down through the ages / David Richard Goldberg.
Description: Springfield, NJ : Gefen Publishing House 2017 | Includes
  bibliographical references.
Identifiers: LCCN 2016001548 | ISBN 9789652298812
Subjects: LCSH: Jews--Biography. | Jewish exempla.
Classification: LCC DS115 .G6155 2017 | DDC 920.0092/924--dc23 LC record
available at https://lccn.loc.gov/2016001548

AMAZING JEWISH HEROES
DOWN THROUGH THE AGES

David Richard Goldberg

gefen publishing house
JERUSALEM ◆ NEW YORK
Est. 1981

Contents
||||||||||||||||||||

Preface...vii

Acknowledgments...xi

Part 1: Amazing Jewish Heroes of Ancient Times

    1. RABBI AKIVA 1

    2. QUEEN ESTHER.. 15

Part 2: Amazing Jewish Heroes of the Early American Wars

    3. HAYM SALOMON 21

    4. URIAH PHILLIPS LEVY 31

Part 3: Amazing Jewish Heroes of the Holocaust

    5. FELIX ZANDMAN.. 39

    6. SIMON WIESENTHAL 59

Part 4: Amazing Jewish Heroes of the State of Israel

    7. THEODOR HERZL... 71

    8. ZE'EV JABOTINSKY.. 75

    9. DAVID BEN-GURION.. 87

    10. GOLDA MEIR 111

    11. MENACHEM BEGIN 139

Conclusion 173

Afterword 181

Resources... 185

Preface
|||||||||||||||||||

I may not be the most religious person of the Hebrew faith in the world. Yes, I pray to Hashem (God) every morning and faithfully recite the daily prayers. Yes, I even take the time to put on tefillin (phylacteries) at least once a week. But lighting Shabbat candles every Friday evening and going to shul diligently on High Holidays (Rosh Hashanah and Yom Kippur) certainly doesn't qualify me as an Orthodox Jew – not even close.

However, I was truly transformed during a recent High Holiday service delivered by our family rabbi, Hershy Bronstein of Coral Springs, Florida. He told the amazing story of Felix Zandman, a Holocaust survivor who, as a teenager, spent seventeen months living in a hole in the ground with three others. How could this happen, I wondered? How could any one person, let alone four people, live that long in what was tantamount to a grave – four feet deep under a gentile friend's bedroom? There was no electricity, no running water, no lighting. There were no toilet facilities! How could anyone function under those conditions, day after day, for that length of time? How could this boy not only survive, but learn mathematics from his uncle, a teacher, while a prisoner underground? How could he not only survive, but go on to graduate from the Sorbonne and became an innovative physicist and world-renowned businessman!

These questions overwhelmed me. What motivated this young boy to survive? What drove him to this level of achievement and success? How did he accomplish so much? Was it a deep belief in God? Was it his dreams for the future? Or was it his spirit of determination, a spirit that would not be squelched? I wondered if he remembered the plight of Joseph, the biblical hero who, millennia ago, languished for twelve years in an Egyptian cell – but survived. Again, how? Was it because he believed in God and he knew he had a higher calling?

So I asked myself, what other Jewish heroes came before and after Felix Zandman? What other Jewish historical figures overcame tremendous obstacles and challenges to achieve greatness in their lives? Certainly Rabbi Akiva – murdered by the Romans in Caesarea around the year 150 CE for being an outspoken advocate of Judaism and the Torah – was another notable Jewish hero. I then learned of many others who have exemplified these heroic attributes, including Moses Montefiore, the nineteenth-century British statesman, businessman, and advocate for Jewish independence and respect worldwide. The list goes on, through to the time of the American Revolutionary War. I was amazed to discover that the revolution was financed, at a most critical juncture in our country's history, by loans generated by Haym Salomon, a financial genius, businessman, patriot, and a Jew. Uriah P. Levy, who was the first Jewish commodore in the United States, endured much antisemitism and was an advocate of the humane treatment of sailors at sea. My hero list was just beginning…

I then thought I should create a compendium of amazing Jewish heroes down through history. These stories should be told so that children of our generation, and adults of all ages, for that matter, could appreciate these Jewish heroes who overcame such great obstacles. I began considering all the Jewish historical figures from biblical times through the twentieth century. Which heroes should I write about? Soon, I decided that my subjects should be historical figures who accomplished much not only for the Jewish people but for the State of Israel too and, ultimately, mankind. Not only were they to be Jewish, but they needed to be believers in God and religious in one way or another. The stories of these heroes show their belief in God and desire to devote their lives to the betterment of mankind by giving light and meaning to the world. Ultimately, the talents, dedication, and accomplishments of these heroes did just that.

Judaism teaches that the world is founded on three tenets: study, work, and acts of loving-kindness (Ethics of the Fathers 1:2). These traditions are taught in even the least observant Jewish homes. The critical thinking and study skills developed through pursuit of Jewish ideals, as well as empathy for those less fortunate, have created a rich incubator for aspiration, ingenuity, and work ethic. How else can we explain the disproportionate number of Jewish scientists, humanitarians, writers, artists, and medical professionals worldwide, who have been major contributors to our world? There are no coincidences here. Thus, in the pages to follow are stories of great Jewish heroes down through the ages – from ancient times to current days – who overcame tremendous obstacles with courage and determination. They have made a difference in history, across time and place; their stories will live forever.

This book was also written to inform my readers, many of whom will be Jewish children and adults lucky enough to live in a free society, what it was to experience the blatant antisemitism endured by heroes like Uriah Phillips Levy, Felix Zandman, Theodor Herzl, and others. These same children most certainly have never known the humiliation of being forced to leave their homeland, like Haym Salomon's family, or the horror of living through the 1930s and 1940s in Europe as a Jew. And they may never really grasp the deep-seated hostility and hatred of a country such as Spain, which fixated on eliminating the Jews as far back as 1492, when the Jewish population that did not convert to Catholicism was expelled.

For this reason I desired these accounts to be written in an easily understood, person-to-person manner – as a "talking book," if you will. It is my hope that young adults of both Jewish and non-Jewish backgrounds discover in the pages that follow relatable and encouraging tales of heroism, and that these stories inspire their own greatness in the here and now.

Acknowledgments
||||||||||||||||||||||||||||||||||||||||||||||

Writing a book about eleven truly amazing people is certainly a challenge, and one cannot as an author do it completely alone. Yes, I was motivated by a visit to Israel three years ago, where I visited truly wondrous historical venues. Certainly I was fascinated by Caesarea and its history, especially as it was the site of Rabbi Akiva's death. But it was the encouragement I received from many friends and associates that really carried me through and motivated me to complete these inspiring stories.

Firstly, great thanks to my brother Leland, who, after I returned from Israel three years ago and excitedly told him of my adventure, said, "So write a book about it!" And I did – *Our Trip to Israel: Memories of a Lifetime*, written in 2013. Then, after a speech during the Jewish High Holidays by my rabbi and good friend Hershy Bronstein about Felix Zandman, I said, "Why don't more people know about his amazing exploits?" The rabbi's response: "David, you should write a book about him, and others as well!" Thus I began to ponder that challenge. Then one night I woke up from a deep slumber and the title appeared in my consciousness – *Amazing Jewish Heroes down through the Ages*. This title definitely came to me from God, I truly believe, and it resonated to my very core – I knew that destiny was calling me to write this book.

So I began, but without the love and support of Janie, my wife of fifty years, I could not have persevered and finished this work. I also have to thank Rabbi Hershy Bronstein, who encouraged me not only at the beginning of this journey, but every step along the way. The rabbi never stopped reminding me of how people young and old, all over the world, would love my book. So, Rabbi, thank you again for your inspiration and guidance.

Colonel Manny Green, a family friend, gave me continual encouragement after reading each chapter. His advice and counsel kept me going when I had moments of doubt.

Certainly one of the important people behind the completion of this book was Stan Silk, a business associate and artist. When I desperately needed photos of my heroes to anchor each chapter, Stan volunteered to do sketches. I did not realize the depth of talent Stan possessed, but after he handed me a sketch of Rabbi Akiva, I knew we were on the right track. Every one of his sketches seems to capture the essence of the individual hero's core. Rabbi Akiva is pensive and thoughtful; Haym Salomon brilliant, soft-spoken, and gentle; Menachem Begin bespectacled but determined. Each character Stan sketched made a deep impression. He was always able to capture that in his work. I can never thank you enough, Stan.

Mr. Guy Gruenberg, another business associate, was always there with a kind word and an inspiring comment. Though born Jewish, Guy admitted he had lost his way in life and strayed from his birthright. When Guy expressed to me that my book and its various stories inspired him to rethink his belief system regarding Judaism, I was totally taken aback. I hope this book will resonate with other readers like Guy, as well.

Lastly, thank you to my son Zachary and his company Forever Studios for compiling and designing a brilliant book concept. Also, kudos to Zachary for helping guide the work from the beginning till the end.

Part 1

AMAZING JEWISH HEROES OF ANCIENT TIMES

1. Rabbi Akiva

||||||||||||||||||||||||||||||||||||||

While on a tour of Israel a few years ago, I stopped at the Roman ruins called Caesarea. I learned that at this very spot, about the year 150 CE, Rabbi Akiva, the beloved and respected sage of Israel, was executed. I wondered who this great rabbi was and why this had happened to him.

The story of Rabbi Akiva[1] begins with the destruction of the Great Temple in Jerusalem in 70 CE. A wealthy landowner named Ben Kalba Savua, who had owned a home in Jerusalem that had been burned down by the Romans, paid the Romans a small fortune to remain a free man and move to a country home for safety. Sadly, he had also lost his wife to illness. But he had a strikingly beautiful daughter, Rachel, who was his only heir and who was possessed of a very keen mind.

Kalba Savua decided to seek out a supervisor to manage his shepherds and vast flocks of sheep. He had no sons to help him in these important tasks, only his daughter Rachel. He sought a loyal, hardworking, honest man who also possessed physical strength – stringent requirements, indeed. He interviewed several candidates, but none measured up until he met a young man recommended by his neighbor, a man named Akiva. Akiva was descended from a heathen family of great nobility who had gone to Jerusalem and converted to Judaism. His parents had lost all their possessions and were then killed during the destruction of Jerusalem and the Great Temple.

---

1 Stories of Rabbi Akiva's life and legacy are sprinkled throughout the Talmud. More recent Jewish writers have authored works compiling these tales as novels. The retelling I present in this chapter takes its inspiration from *Akiva* by Marcus Lehmann (Nanuet, NY: Feldheim, 2003), with permission from the copyright holder.

1

At this time, Kalba Savua's daughter Rachel appeared and announced a visitor to their home who said he intended to be her husband. She left without commenting on Akiva. Kalba Savua then asked Akiva if, and under what conditions, he would be willing to be employed by him. "I will ask you to pay me what I am worth – you will not underpay me," was his response.

With that, he was hired on the spot and given the role of grand supervisor of Kalba Savua's vast holdings. When Akiva was asked about Judaism, and the proper treatment of animals according to Judaic law, he explained his ignorance in the Torah and the laws, but he was employed nevertheless.

Soon after, a great discussion occurred in Kalba Savua's home. The suitor he had handpicked to marry his daughter expressed the opinion that the Jews would be better off merging with the Roman Empire! Kalba Savua's daughter Rachel admonished him, strongly defending Israel and the Jewish Torah and traditions, to her father's delight. Kalba Savua also learned that Akiva's previous employer was a poor man whose son had run away to study the Torah and later became a learned rabbi. When this man's son, the rabbi, came home to visit, he had been impressed with Akiva's sharp mind and wisdom, and he encouraged Akiva to go to study Torah, but Akiva had adamantly refused.

Kalba Savua's daughter Rachel heard every word of this discussion and wondered if she could influence Akiva where the rabbi had failed. She was now interested – very much so.

As fate would have it, not long after these events, the great rabbi Yohanan Ben Zakkai died. This great teacher and pillar of strength was sorely missed by the Jews. When word of Rabbi Yohanan's passing reached Rachel, she became distraught and saddened. Because she cared so deeply for her Judaism and her God, she worried over the future of Israel and its people. Since she was the daughter of a wealthy man, she had all of the luxuries and jewelry she would ever want or need, yet still her very core, her soul, would not be content until a new great rabbi emerged. She prayed for a man of great character, intelligence, and dedication.

Rachel thought of the poor shepherd Akiva. Could he be influenced to change his thinking about his Jewish faith?

Rachel decided to seek out Akiva in the pastures where he was tending the flocks of sheep. He had not heard of the death of the great Rabbi Yohanan and could not have cared less. For whatever reason, he disliked rabbis deeply, calling them out for not really being interested in the Jewish people's welfare. He even felt the Jews were responsible for the Romans' destruction of Israel and its great Temple! Rachel listened intently to all Akiva had to say. When he had finished, she countered, "Jews were the Chosen People, who have been given the Torah by God, and that legacy must be continued for coming generations. We must see to it that the Torah is not forgotten, that Israel is not stripped of its greatest treasure!"

Rachel was determined to get through to Akiva. "My dear shepherd, you are not a typical man of the field. You have great intelligence and character, traits found in the great men of Israel," Rachel continued, "I would love to see you begin to learn about the teachings of the Torah, and you too someday could achieve that greatness I speak of!" Akiva listened carefully now, and Rachel's words were beginning to penetrate his very heart and soul. *Maybe*, he thought, *I really should think about her poignant words*. Akiva began saying his daily prayers with greater concentration, as Rachel had made him realize his ignorance of the prayers' meaning and significance. Now questions arose in his mind, questions not easily answered. He was motivated to educate himself, to inquire, to learn about his neglected Judaism.

Rachel was at a crossroads in her life and contemplated her fate while walking through the lush gardens on her father's estate. She had lost her mother when she was young, and she had no brothers or sisters. The only servant she was close to had died a year before, and her childhood friends had perished in the Roman war, or had been sold as slaves. Thus Rachel was often lonely, very lonely. Even her father, who truly loved her, was often aloof and uncommunicative. This beautiful young girl was all by herself in the world, completely alone. Then, out of the blue, our shepherd Akiva appeared. He too had been contemplating his fate, his life, for days. He told Rachel of his need to find answers to the many questions that occupied his mind, his wish to learn more about Judaism, Torah, his people, their traditions, and their fate. "Rachel, I have so many questions that I have been pondering about Judaism, the Torah, my people and their traditions. I must find answers and satisfy this thirst for knowledge now – because of you!"

Rachel thought, and answered softly: "Some people strive for greatness through acquiring knowledge by study. That effort is not easy. It entails great sacrifice and even suffering. Most uneducated people don't need that goal. They are happy with their station in life. But the strivers, the doers take on a heavy mantle of responsibility, because Israel has been God's chosen people, and has incurred great suffering and pain. Always, though, God has been there for us, bringing us back from disasters, back to firm ground – we will always prevail. We must prevail!" Rachel now looked at Akiva pensively and awaited his response.

At first Akiva, this very strong, handsome young shepherd, was very quiet, very thoughtful. But then he looked at Rachel with wonder and amazement. He knew in his heart her words were true. He also felt that her sage, divine comments had inspired him deeply. He spoke again to her: "Why has God allowed so many bad things to happen to the Jewish people?" Rachel thought for a minute and now implored Akiva, "You should learn about Torah and our God and then you will find the answer to your question." Akiva then asked Rachel another question about the Torah. This time she pointed out a stream running nearby. "Akiva," she blurted out, "the water from that gushing stream is being blocked and impeded by those big rocks you see in the middle of the water. But over the years, the water's flow has worn these rocks down with its constant splashing and motion against them – yes, little droplets of water against the high, strong stones have done that!"

Akiva was astounded – Rachel's analogy spoke directly to his deepest thoughts and beliefs about his Jewish faith. He felt for several moments that in the whole world there were no other words than hers, no other person but Rachel. Finally, Rachel said to him, "No more questions, Akiva. You must go and learn – learn!"

Our shepherd Akiva stood pondering his fate. He was also very lonely, without friends or family. What would his future be like alone?

He then wondered about Jewish history and the role of women, particularly about the Hebrews' four hundred years of slavery in Egypt. He continued to question Rachel, now on the role of women in that unfortunate period of slavery. She again was specific in her reply. "Akiva, if it weren't for the women of Egypt's Jews – the wives and mothers – our people would not have persevered, would have faded into history! The vibrancy of Jewish life is the Jewish home and the wives who kept families and hopes and dreams alive!"

Akiva blurted out: "If only I could find a wife who would stand by me like that, then I would happily dedicate my life to Torah study, even if I was poor and had nothing." He looked at Rachel, and he said, "Someone like you, Rachel, my master's daughter, whom I would never reproach." Rachel responded with clarity and passion: "If I knew that one day you would become a great teacher of Israel – I would not turn you down!"

Akiva was stunned! He was overjoyed beyond words at this turn of events – this beautiful, brilliant, devoted, wonderful daughter of his master had agreed to be his wife. He also felt uncertainty, however, deeming himself unworthy of the status he would enjoy as Rachel's husband. He was, in truth, at this moment a poor shepherd.

Akiva was certainly confused over what to do next, but Rachel had asked him to speak to her father about their plans. So one day, when Kalba Savua, his employer, approached and complimented him on his good work, he asked Kalba Savua to release him from his duties, to go and study the Torah. He explained: "Your daughter has promised to marry me if I do!"

Kalba Savua was astonished and perplexed, and he immediately sent for his daughter to confirm this crazy story. As a loving father, he had never placed restrictions on Rachel in any way; they had always agreed on everything, including the suitor he had suggested for her. They had rejected him together. So Kalba Savua started by saying he disbelieved Akiva, that Akiva was poor, of pagan stock, and utterly ignorant – "Why would you marry this man?" he asked Rachel. She defended Akiva, citing his brilliant mind and intellectual abilities, and her belief that he could become one of Israel's greatest teachers. But Kalba Savua was not convinced, suspecting that Akiva was only interested in the family's wealth.

Rachel finally stated that if they were poor together, she would work, would dedicate herself to her husband, would do whatever was needed to survive with him. She proudly pronounced, "Akiva will be a blessing to our people, as the greatest rabbis have been; he will teach them and fulfill the prophecy." But Kalba Savua was still not convinced, and ordered Akiva to leave his house that same day. Rachel then implored her father: "I have given my word to Akiva, I will keep it, I will never marry anyone else!"

With that, Kalba Savua, in a rage, disowned his daughter, and ordered her to leave his house with only the clothing she was wearing! Rachel was now totally distraught; she was deeply hurt by her father's reaction.

Her future with Akiva was fated – she would be the poor wife of a rabbinical student. What a decision for a wealthy young woman to make! She was convinced that her new husband would achieve greatness as a rabbi of Israel, and she knew she was sacrificing her comfortable life, her own father, and her future as an heiress. All this because of her belief that the Jewish people could not survive without a great rabbi to lead them at that moment in history, and that Akiva could be that leader. She was a proud Jewess, a great admirer of the Torah, and a strong believer in God's promise to the Jewish people. She was now willing to throw everything away for the noble purpose of marrying Akiva.

Now husband and wife, and alone in the world except for each other, Rachel and Akiva bought a small hut in the town of Gimzo. Rachel used the fine clothing and jewelry she had been wearing when driven from her beloved father's house to buy their home. Now she, by herself, approached one of the great sages of Israel, Rabbi Nachum. He could not believe that she had forsaken her father and his comforts.

After hearing about her desire to have her husband dedicate himself to Torah study, he complimented her bravery and said, "You deserve to see your husband become a Torah scholar and great teacher of Israel. Your self-sacrifice will be praised by our people for thousands of years, and you will be a role model for the women of Israel."

With that, Akiva was brought to the rabbi. When the rabbi was told that Akiva could not read or write Hebrew, he was flabbergasted. He agreed to teach Akiva, but warned him that it would not be easy. Rachel went home to their hut and began spinning cloth to support them.

After the first day of study, Akiva came home and told Rachel what he had learned. He said that he had learned to read and write the letters of the alphabet, and the significance and value of each letter. He continued by stating that he had begun reading the Holy Torah, and had been encouraged to ask any question, without embarrassment. After an in-depth discussion of his progress in learning Hebrew, and the meaning of God's letters in the Torah, Rachel was impressed. Showing her happiness, she reiterated her belief to him that he would become a great teacher.

Akiva continued to advance in his studies. He was becoming a deep Torah thinker, and his reputation was growing quickly. His love and thirst for learning amazed everyone. But his quest for knowledge was not only limited to the Torah – doctors, astronomers, and linguists were all sources from whom he desired to learn. Rabbi Nachum taught Akiva a great deal, even taking him to Rome as his assistant and prize pupil. There they impressed many Roman officers with Judaism and their belief in one God. Akiva received gifts from the emperor as well, which helped with his family's modest needs.

Soon after, the great Rabbi Nachum died of an illness. Akiva then yearned to go to the great center of Torah study, Yavneh. This would be a wonderful place to study – there, the wellspring of Torah knowledge flowed; many great rabbis had learned and taught in that place.

When Akiva arrived at Yavneh alone, he found it to be very strict and discovered that he still fell below the high standards of holiness and purity expected there. Scholastically, he was also the butt of critical comments and derision. Although Akiva was heavily reprimanded and suffered much punishment, he never wavered, despite these setbacks.

Akiva persevered, and soon his great intellect was recognized by his rabbinical teachers. But still, he was afraid to speak up in this setting of great scholars. For twelve years, he sat like a mute at the feet of his teachers, without saying a word! But he was absorbing all the knowledge imparted to him, and in private was clarifying this wisdom for his own understanding.

Finally, after those first twelve years, Akiva felt confident enough to express his views on various subjects, including matters of the laws of Sabbath. Soon, other subjects were discussed, and it became obvious to teachers and students alike that Akiva's vast knowledge, deep understanding, keen analytical mind, and phenomenal memory qualified him as a great rabbi himself. Thereafter, even the younger students began to follow him and his teachings. He had finally arrived!

But Rabbi Akiva had not seen his wife or children for twelve long years. He visited the house just once over the years, and at that time he overheard his wife Rachel defending him from a neighbor's criticism over his long absence. "I consented to his being away for so long," Rachel said. "If he becomes a great teacher, I would accept his absence even longer!" Knowing that he had her approval, Akiva left without even seeing his beloved wife.

Akiva did not see his wife again until he returned home after twelve years with thousands of disciples in tow. People were streaming from all over to see this renowned scholar. Rachel had heard he was coming. Joyous and fearful at the same time, she finally saw him in the midst of the crowd. She attempted to push toward him, but was blocked by his pupils. Akiva saw her and cried out her name. "Leave her alone!" he commanded. "If not for her, I would have remained an ignorant shepherd. All my Torah and all your Torah are hers!" With that, they clung to each other. They were together again after so many long years.

Our story returns now to Rachel's father, Ben Kalba Savua, who had rejected Rachel and her husband many years before. He had not allowed them back into his life, rejecting all their attempts at reconciliation. He was now old and lonely and felt his time was nearing an end. He wanted his wealth to be used for charity, but did not know where to turn. So what did he do? He went and consulted with a great rabbi who lived nearby – unbeknownst to him, this was none other than our hero. When Kalba Savua was finally in Rabbi Akiva's presence, he did not recognize his former employee. He asked for Rabbi Akiva's advice on how best to leave his estate.

"Do you have any children?" the rabbi asked.

Kalba Savua answered that he indeed had one daughter, but she had married a poor, ignorant shepherd and he had disowned her.

Rabbi Akiva then asked him, "Say that poor shepherd had become a Torah scholar. Had you known this would be his destiny, would you have done the same thing? If he had become a man greatly renowned for his knowledge and learning – someone like myself, for example?"

Kalba Savua exclaimed, "I would have considered myself very fortunate if my daughter had chosen someone like you!"

Rabbi Akiva could not maintain the charade any longer. "I am Akiva Ben Yosef, my dear father," he cried out. "I was that shepherd, and your daughter Rachel is my cherished wife!" Kalba Savua could neither believe his ears nor control his emotions. He began to weep. "Can you forgive me, Rabbi?" he sobbed uncontrollably, a broken old man. But Rabbi Akiva was kind to him: "Your actions were justified, so I will nullify your vow as if it never was. Had you known what the future held, you would not have taken that vow!"

With that, Kalba Savua implored the great rabbi to share his house and his wealth with him immediately. When Rachel was finally summoned, she entered the room where they were, saw her father, and fell to the floor and embraced him. Kalba Savua gently lifted her up and hugged and kissed her, saying, "You foresaw the future better than I. Forgive me for these years of suffering I have caused you!"

But Rachel was not to be denied. "Suffering? How could I have suffered when I was married to the wisest and most noble man on earth? I am fortunate and happy. All I missed was your love, Father." Kalba Savua was overjoyed with this turn of events. No longer would he be lonely in his old age.

Rabbi Akiva became renowned not only for his wisdom, but now for his wealth as well. What did he do first? He purchased a golden crown with a sketch of the city of Jerusalem engraved on it for his beloved Rachel; he had promised it to her when they were poor. Now Rachel, always modest and pious, wore the crown out of pride and joy. This was an example to the daughters of Israel that great things can be accomplished through a woman's self-sacrifice and devotion to her husband and religion.

Even though they saw each other infrequently while Rabbi Akiva continued to grow into a great rabbi, both Akiva and Rachel had a wonderful, loving marriage. It is sad to say that Rachel, Rabbi Akiva's rock, the love of his life and his inspiration, died when she was in her seventies, leaving him alone with his many followers.

Our hero Akiva's life took many incredible twists and turns, and he was particularly involved with the Roman persecution of the Jewish people. Twice he made the long trek by sea to Rome, where he encountered unremitting animosity toward the Jews.

During the first visit, he had impressed the emperor so much that the emperor had bestowed gifts upon him, which allowed him to provide a better life for his family.

Rabbi Akiva's rise to prominence as a Jewish leader took him to Rome once more, this time as the guest of a notable Roman citizen. There, Akiva discovered that Emperor Domitian planned to destroy all the Jews in his realm, many of whom were Romans who had converted to Judaism. Domitian was determined to protect the old Roman gods from the perceived threat. Jews were forbidden from traveling out of the city. Akiva found out that a relative of the emperor was also to be slain for his sympathies for the Jews of Rome, so Flavius Clemens, a Roman patriarch and member of the secret council, was going to speak out for the Jewish people – but he was rebuffed. Finally, Flavius Clemens was sentenced to death for decrying the evil decree regarding the Jews. Time passed, and on Yom Kippur, the decree against the Jews was to be renewed. All of Rome's Jews were frightened, but as fate would have it, Emperor Domitian was assassinated by a fellow Roman. The new emperor was respectful of the Jews, and Rabbi Akiva and his party were allowed to leave Rome for Judea.

Since Jews were dispersed throughout the Roman Empire at this time (around 100 CE), Rabbi Akiva took it upon himself to travel to faraway places to unite the Jewish people. His warning to his fellow Jews was to not rebel against the Roman power, but to wait for the help of other subjugated nations and the Redeemer (a king; *moshiach*). So, his first journey was to Alexandria, Egypt, where Jewish religious traditions had waned. The community in Alexandria was not observing the Sabbath or the holidays, and not keeping kosher. After speaking to the most prominent Jew in Alexandria, and hearing his justification for this behavior, Rabbi Akiva asked to address the Jewish community in the great synagogue. There, ten thousand filled the hall to capacity.

Akiva began by saying, "My brothers, our forefathers were once slaves here, and God took them out with a strong hand. He brought them to Mount Sinai and said, 'I am the Lord your God. You shall not have other gods before Me.' But you invoke the names of the Greek gods, and you eat impure animals, and have become like the Romans." He went on to remind them of their neglect of the study of the Torah. Finally, he implored them to forsake their wicked ways: "Return to God that He may have mercy on you and save you!"

The people wept after this impassioned speech, but the Jewish leaders in Alexandria continued to lead the people down the path of the pagans, away from proper Jewish teachings and observance. Later, the uprising Akiva had warned against destroyed the Jewish community in Egypt and other places. His warnings had gone unheeded by his fellow Jews.

Rabbi Akiva and the Jewish sages of that time believed that no revolt against the Roman Empire could succeed without a *moshiach*.

With that in mind, it came to Akiva's attention that a certain remarkable man, an orphan and a learned Torah scholar, possessed messianic-like qualities. When Rabbi Akiva finally met Bar Koziva, he was impressed with his noble bearing and demeanor. Akiva endorsed Bar Koziva and renamed him Bar Kochba – "the Star." Bar Kochba and his Judean army drove the Romans away from Judea and Galilee. With 200,000 infantry troops, thirty thousand bowmen, and twenty thousand horsemen, Bar Kochba defeated the Romans and killed their general, Paulus Martius. A second Roman attack was repressed, and the Roman second-in-command was killed as well. Thirty thousand Romans were dead; Rabbi Akiva praised God Almighty for the victory.

Bar Kochba seemed invincible, but Emperor Hadrian then sent his best general, Severus, to Judea with a mighty army. All of Judea, except Jerusalem, was now in Jewish hands, so in his last battle, Bar Kochba liberated the Holy City, Jerusalem. Upon this great victory, Rabbi Akiva spoke at the podium on Mount Moriah. He spoke of rebuilding the Third Temple and making it more beautiful than ever. Akiva proclaimed the military victory as the advent of God's promised eternal peace and reconstruction of the Jewish land and Temple, citing the prophet Zechariah's words: "I return unto Zion and will dwell in the midst of Jerusalem" (8:3).

Soon, however, Bar Kochba alienated Rabbi Akiva by aligning his army with the Samaritans, or Kusim. Akiva had pleaded with him to trust in God's infinite power, but Bar Kochba insisted he could defeat the Romans without God's assistance! Bar Kochba threatened to kill Akiva for challenging him, but stopped short and sent him away instead. Once more after that, Bar Kochba pleaded with Akiva to join him in his quest, and once more the rabbi repeated that trust in God's name and God's prophecy would sanctify his name. Akiva finally left Bar Kochba and, now a hundred years old, went back to teaching his students.

The Romans continued to march on Judea, taking back one city after another. Finally, Bar Kochba's Samaritan allies turned against him. He had killed his own uncle in anger, and now he faced defeat. He realized too late that Rabbi Akiva's warnings were correct: he should not have relied on the Samaritans. Astonishingly, Bar Kochba met his end by being suffocated by a huge snake! But the Jewish people fought on. In Beitar, 580,000 Jews – men, women, and children – died. The Romans, under Hadrian, lost many soldiers as well and were angry with this Jewish uprising.

The Temple had been destroyed a second time – and all Jewish observance was forbidden. But the Jews would not yield to this edict, and they vowed to continue their Torah study. Rabbi Akiva, now 119 years old, was still teaching – ever aware and mentally alert, and as youthful as ever. But the Romans had spies everywhere, and one day Akiva and his new wife Rufina were arrested. She had been the wife of Tineius Rufus, a Roman general, and had converted to Judaism of her own volition to marry Rabbi Akiva. When given the choice of freedom in exchange for remarrying her former husband, she refused. With that, Tineius Rufus threatened to torture Rabbi Akiva to death. Rufina then said to Tineius Rufus: "Rabbi Akiva will happily give his life for God and the Holy Torah. This is what he has lived for."

Akiva, in a prison in the Roman coastal city Caesarea, rationed his water so he could wash his hands and pray according to his religious observance. This left very little to drink, so one of his students paid the warden to supply our hero with more water, to both wash and drink.

Rufina had been ordered to see Tineius Rufus daily. He begged her to remarry him, until finally, after he threatened her with harsh measures, she replied passionately, "I will always be Rabbi Akiva's wife, in purity and sanctity, until the end of my life; and if I am separated from him now, we will surely be reunited in the world of eternal bliss!" With that, she killed herself with a dagger!

Tinieus Rufus was furious; he then decided to end Rabbi Akiva's life. It was dawn on Yom Kippur, the holiest day in the Jewish calendar. At 120 years old, Rabbi Akiva was still strong, his mind clear, his spirit unbroken. He was tied to a stake. Guards took burning tongs and began to tear pieces of flesh from his body. Rabbi Akiva was in excruciating pain, but remained silent and reflective.

The day was breaking, the sun rising above the hills in the east. Our hero put his hand over his eyes, and called out loudly, "Hear, O Israel! The Lord our God, the Lord is One! Blessed be His name, Whose kingdom is for ever and ever! And you shall love the Lord your God with all your heart, and with all your soul, and with all your might!"

And as his students drew closer to him, he continued to recite, "*Shema Yisrael, A-do-nai E-lo-heinu, A-do-nai Echad!*" (Hear, O Israel! The Lord our God, the Lord is One!). With that, he died.

Akiva's body was taken to a cave in the mountains by his followers, and the entrance was sealed forever. Rabbi Akiva died a martyr and has remained the symbol of Jewish optimism and hope throughout the ages of exile and despair. His faith in a better tomorrow for Jews (and all humanity) and his upbeat outlook on life despite adversities never wavered. His example is for all generations of Jews to see, a great dawn of hope for future generations. Rabbi Akiva, the ultimate Jewish outsider, who descended from Jewish converts, has become the ultimate hero, not just to converts and the uneducated, who may draw inspiration from his journey from humble beginnings to meteoric accomplishments, but to Jews for all time.

Rest in peace, our hero Rabbi Akiva. We will never forget you.

2. Queen Esther
||||||||||||||||||||||||||||||||||||||||||||

The name Esther is related to the Hebrew word *hester*, meaning "hidden."[2] Queen Esther, a Jewess by birth, served as queen to King Ahasuerus (Xerxes) of Persia but guarded the secret of her ancestry for years. At a turning point for the welfare of the Jews, Esther came out of hiding and bravely stood up for her people. So how did this beautiful Jewish woman become the queen of Persia? How did she save the Jewish people and become an amazing heroine? And how was it that this young woman was picked to be the king's new bride, over all the beautiful young candidates from all the provinces of Persia, when she disdained makeup and beauty treatments, didn't dress in the most exquisite clothing (which the others requested), and according to some commentaries wasn't even the most physically beautiful of the assembled maidens? Why, then, was she chosen? Esther was humble and behaved with marked respect and deference; Esther enchanted everyone with her modesty *as well as* her beauty. Her beauty radiated from her inner self, imbuing her with special grace and charm that were hers alone.

Who was Esther, this young woman with these strange, special charms? The orphaned daughter of Avichayil, Esther was raised by her cousin Mordechai, who adopted her as his own. Mordechai was a member of the Sanhedrin (the Jewish Supreme Court) and a Torah sage. Being raised in the home of a man dedicated to study of the laws of Torah certainly would have influenced young Esther's refined personal character.

Surprisingly, the selection of a queen of Persia to replace the banished Vashti took several years. But after the king spent one night with

---

2 The information presented in this chapter is drawn from the Midrashim and traditional exegesis on the Book of Esther as explained in the resources listed at the end of this volume.

Esther, he fell in love and decided to make her his new queen. The new Queen Esther did not want to reveal her religion to the king, as Mordechai had requested of her, so for nine years, Esther practiced Judaism in secret. Her handpicked Jewish servants provided her with kosher food and helped her keep the Sabbath. These same servants were also duty-bound to keep Queen Esther's secret – for nine years!

So how did this happen? Why would a beautiful young Jewish woman devote years of her life to living a lie in the palace of a non-Jewish king? Did Mordechai see something unique in Esther, something that might evolve into an opportunity to save the Jewish people? Did Mordechai know of any antisemitic sentiments King Ahasuerus might have? Did he fear an impending disaster for Persia's Jewish population?

The events that followed will not be new to readers familiar with the Book of Esther. Mordechai saved Ahasuerus's life by discovering and foiling a plot to poison his drink. Then came Haman, the king's viceroy, who demanded that all citizenry should bow down before him. But Mordechai refused, saying he bowed to no one but God. This angered Haman, and he secured a decree from the king that called for the massacre of all Persia's Jews. This decision escaped the king's best judgment, and it alarmed Mordechai greatly.

Mordechai told Esther of the genocide that had been ordered by her husband, the king. What could she do to help? Upon the threat of death, no one was allowed to appear before the king unannounced, not even his own queen! Yet Mordechai pointed out to her that it was perhaps to fulfill this very purpose that she had found herself in the position of queen. Queen Esther, together with her servants and all the Jews of her city, Shushan (Susa), fasted and prayed for three days. Finally, she appeared before the king in his court, risking her life. Thankfully, the king loved her deeply and reached out to her and asked her what she desired. What did she request? A dinner for three – the king, Haman, and herself!

Haman and the king enjoyed themselves immensely at the banquet Esther threw in their honor. During the festivities, Ahasuerus again asked Queen Esther what she desired; Esther answered that she wanted nothing more than the presence of Ahasuerus and Haman at another banquet, the following night. What a wise woman! Haman at this point was feeling mighty full of himself. He felt that his seat of influence in the royal household was secured. Ahasuerus surely wondered what his wife's preoccupation with the viceroy was about.

At the second banquet, the king again asked Esther what she desired. This time she was prepared to give him a true answer. This was a crucial moment in Esther's life – she had deliberately hidden her Jewishness from her king for nine years, and now she had to ask him to spare the lives of her people, her fellow Jews – admitting that she also was a Jewess!

But she did so, requesting that the king spare her and her people from the man who wanted them all killed – with Haman standing right there in the same room! King Ahasuerus realized Haman's treachery and stormed from the hall in a rage. Haman beseeched the queen to save his life and fell upon her couch – a serious affront to the king, who happened to return at that moment! Ahasuerus feared that Haman intended to molest Esther, his queen, whom he loved despite finally learning her true heritage.

Our story ends with Haman being hanged on the very gallows he had prepared for Mordechai. And Mordechai was then appointed to be the new viceroy of the Persian kingdom! Wow! An amazing turnaround.

Queen Esther and Mordechai together saved the Jews of Persia from extermination by Haman, a bitter antisemite. Our queen became an icon and is now considered one of the most heroic women in Jewish history. Her story, which she ordered to be written down and preserved as part of Jewish history, is repeated every year during the Jewish holiday of Purim. Esther was an amazing woman who risked her life to save many Jews. Her incredible story has truly endured down through the ages.[3]

---

3   A structure known as the "Tomb of Esther and Mordechai" can be found in Hamadan, modern-day Iran. The village Kfar Bar'am, in northern Israel, also claims to be the burial place of Queen Esther.

Part 2

AMAZING JEWISH HEROES OF THE EARLY AMERICAN WARS

3. Haym Salomon
||||||||||||||||||||||||||||||||||||||||||||||

W hen General George Washington sat around the strategy table with his staff of officers shortly before the final revolutionary battle at Yorktown, the Continental Army was in dire straits. The soldiers were ragged and hungry, and the units were short of arms, ammunition, and supplies. Even the most dedicated among them were beginning to abandon hope. Washington had conceived a brilliant plan to surprise the British forces at Yorktown from two sides at once. His staff enthusiastically embraced this strategy, but they lacked the money to carry out the grand plan. His army, once twenty thousand strong, had by now been reduced to nine thousand men, and there was no more federal money or federal credit to support the troops. Washington had already spent every cent he could raise and much of his own fortune as well, and had even borrowed beyond the limits of his personal credit. The deficit totaled twenty thousand dollars.

"Now we must send for Haym Salomon!" Washington commanded. Every officer at the table knew that the destiny of the fledgling nation might very well depend on a swift and successful consultation with Salomon, a major financier of the American Revolution – and a Jew.

Haym Salomon was born in 1740 in Lesno, Poland, of transplanted Sephardic (Spanish) Jewish parents. Early in his childhood in Poland, Haym's facility with languages was recognized, and he later mastered six: English, Polish, German, French, Italian, and Russian. Haym was also actively involved in Jewish studies, and his family observed of all the Jewish holidays and festivities. He also exhibited an overwhelming desire to live in a free society.

At the tender age of twenty, Haym left his home under Poland's overbearing monarchy and traveled about Europe learning the business of banking. He was a quick study and became very skilled in brokering goods and services. Eventually he made his way to England and then sailed to New York City in 1772. Historians believe Salomon was the first Jew of Polish birth to emigrate to America, joining the three thousand Jewish colonists who had preceded him.

Thus Salomon opened offices in New York in 1773 as a merchant broker, using borrowed money, and immediately prospered in his new venture. He also soon identified with the Sons of Liberty, a colonial secret society formed in protest to the Stamp Act of 1765. This association was to get Haym in very serious trouble, but our hero was determined to do whatever was needed to help his adopted country.

A little more personal detail about Haym: he was a rather small, soft-spoken man with a gentle bearing. His manner and speech reflected his European background. And since he dealt with other immigrants and was able to communicate with many diverse parties in his business dealings because of his talent for languages, he was in high demand.

His association with the Sons of Liberty was an easy choice. He had left Poland to live as a free man and was determined for America to be his homeland. Soon Haym was keeping company with a young Alexander Hamilton, John Lamb, and other notable anti-British colonists. Not long after, on July 4, 1776, the United States ratified its Declaration of Independence from Great Britain. Our hero was elated.

The declaration triggered a chain of events resulting in British troops, under Sir William Howe, taking control of New York City in September 1776. Five days later, however, the city was in flames, and the British suspected the Sons of Liberty as the culprits responsible for the arson. Its members, including Haym Salomon, were hunted down and imprisoned.

The jail was an ancient warehouse with a leaky roof, no heating, and only rudimentary medical facilities. Very soon, however, Haym was moved to a maximum-security prison designed to hold those prisoners condemned to death. It was called the Provost and featured a warden who regularly mistreated and starved thousands of inmates to death. In addition, there were no windows and thus no ventilation, and there was only a single toilet for a large number of men – horrible conditions in any civilization. Haym had already developed a bad cold and was suffering from severe chest pains. Avoiding possible hanging or starvation was his prime motivation – he must live! So what was Haym to do?

He soon became aware that the Hessian (German) guards were not happy campers. They had been drafted by the British and were far away from their homes and families. Since the British did not speak German, they had problems communicating with the Hessians. Haym made his talent for languages known to the British, and they soon moved him to a more comfortable cell where he was at last able to breathe fresh air. His health improved, and he finally felt alive again! Thank God!

Haym discovered that the state of Pennsylvania, in an unbelievable effort to neutralize the enemy's strength, was offering one hundred acres of free farmland to Hessians who deserted the British and remained peaceful. Our hero now had a plan of action. Haym cautiously approached the younger guards, those without families back home, with news of this opportunity for freedom. He was taking a huge risk, for he could have been hanged, or worse. The Germans were also naturally suspicious of his offer – what if he was trying to trick them into joining the Continental Army?

History records that Haym was a very persuasive salesman for Pennsylvania and freedom – because he was personally responsible for hundreds of German desertions in just a few months. The British never knew who was behind it. If they had known, the history of the United States would certainly have played out very differently.

Haym survived by his guile and wits, continuously outwitting his British captors. Soon, almost miraculously, because of his skills as a German interpreter for the British, he was released from prison – on parole, of course – and he was determined to start anew.

From that point forward, Haym's personal life took a turn for the better. He was a free man. He opened new offices in New York

City, closer to the center of commerce. He also wooed and married Rachel Franks, the daughter of a successful and respected Philadelphia merchant. He was thirty-six and she was but fifteen years of age (a twenty-one-year difference), but fortunately this marriage came with a great dividend for Haym. Rachel's father and uncle were both successful businessmen who enjoyed a great reputation in dealings with the Germans and the British. So naturally, Haym, the son-in-law of Mr. Moses Franks, became a merchant providing goods and provisions to the British troops as well as sailing vessels docked at the port of New York.

With these contacts and his knowledge of finance, Haym began to prosper tremendously in his new venture. But he also continued his secret work with the Sons of Liberty, convincing German soldiers to desert and join the colonies. These actions were indeed dangerous, for they were treacherous acts in the eyes of the British. Haym's passion, his love of liberty, again overrode all other concerns. The British never suspected the "small, mannerly, brown-eyed Jew" of being much of a threat to His Majesty's army.[4]

Haym persisted in this work because the British still occupied colonists' homes and denied them freedom of speech and personal liberties. He persisted in spite of his deteriorating health; the cough he had contracted in prison had developed into tuberculosis.

The British soon suspected Haym to be a secret agent, however, and arrested him again in 1778. This time, after being taken to the Provost in New York City, whence prisoners never returned, he was charged with being a spy. There was no jury, and Haym did not have a lawyer. There was certainly no appeals process. Sadly, this brave man, who had just become a father, was condemned to be hanged the very next day at sunrise! This was British "justice" at its worst! Now, Haym knew that because of his illness he would not live to a ripe old age, and so he felt compelled to accomplish great things with every minute of his time left. What should he do? He had to live; he must survive!

---

4   Vick Knight Jr., *Send for Haym Salomon!* (Alhambra, CA: Borden Publishing Co./Haym Salomon Foundation, 1976).

How many people in this scenario would feel that all was lost, that there was no hope? Feeling doomed, they would despair of ever seeing their spouses or families again. But Haym was not like that; he was an enterprising and clever man, even under great stress. He always planned ahead and was usually well prepared for any crisis he might face. He had always known that, sooner or later, he would be arrested, so he was armed – not with a gun but with gold coins concealed in his clothing. During the long night, Haym bribed one or more of the guards to gain his freedom. Certainly, his knowledge of German and his powers of persuasion, not to mention the gold bribe, paid off. He was free again, but where to go now? What to do?

Haym made his way out of New York, but he was penniless and without friends or family. He had learned from Alexander MacDougall, a leader of the Sons of Liberty and the Continental army, that the army needed food and clothing. So he decided to go to Philadelphia and set out on the 160-mile journey on foot. He must have been terribly lonely – he was leaving behind his family in New York – but he was going to fulfill his destiny.

In August 1778, Philadelphia was a city alive, bustling with activity. Its waterfront was the hub of trade, and ships of all kinds, foreign and domestic, loaded and unloaded their cargoes at its docks. When Haym finally arrived, he had to start somewhere, and so, an observant Jew, he sought out the local synagogue and its congregants. He soon made friends and business contacts and also became a broker for supplies and bills of exchange. His family connections were certainly a great asset in his new environs, and his knowledge of foreign and domestic commerce, along with his ability to speak several languages, were also great advantages for him in business.

Fortunately, his wife Rachel and his son Ezekiel were able to join him in Philadelphia not long after. He had lost his New York home, a fortune of thirty thousand dollars (millions in today's currency), and his business, but he had his family back. Surely his deep belief in God had brought him renewed happiness and vigor to continue his work.

His health worsened, however. He was coughing heavily because of the tuberculosis and was told by his doctor to slow down. But instead he was spurred to do even more with the time he had left! Haym established himself in Philadelphia with his highly specialized skills, the exchange of foreign currencies to negotiable instruments. His honesty and efficiency were soon noticed by the French foreign minister, and he became paymaster for the French army and navy in America; in addition to this very prestigious position, he also made loans to French ambassadors.

History records that Haym came at this point to the attention of Robert Morris, United States minister of finance under General Washington. Morris sought out Salomon's help after running into problems negotiating with the French on bills of exchange and ended up bringing him aboard to broker currency exchanges that favored the federal government. Working with Morris, Haym came to know that Washington's army was badly in need of money. This opportunity, with Morris, would allow Haym to make a contribution to America by using the negotiating talents he had developed – and to ultimately fulfill his destiny. It is recorded in Robert Morris's diary that between 1781 and 1784 Haym Salomon lent more than $200,000 to the government – our hero Salomon provided the money to feed Washington's troops and support his military campaign.[5]

In addition to helping support the military, Haym Salomon's generosity extended to making loans to important historical figures such as James Madison, the author of the Constitution and a two-term president (Salomon was Madison's private benefactor). Haym's extensive loans to Thomas Jefferson, John Paul Jones, Governor Thomas Mifflin (of Pennsylvania), James Wilson (signatory of the Declaration of Independence), President James Monroe, and many other individuals of note are documented in the Library of Congress. Haym could not say no to these great Americans, who helped kick-start the fledgling colonies.

---

5   "Haym Salomon: American Financier and Patriot," *Encyclopaedia Britannica*, https://www.britannica.com/biography/Haym-Salomon.

It is important to note that these cash "loans" were made with no interest, or minimal interest, even though Haym was aware they might not be repaid for a long time. Haym firmly believed in Washington's victory and placed his entire fortune at the general's disposal, even supporting whole regiments of the Continental Army. What a man, at such a crucial time in American history! There aren't many patriots, even in contemporary times, who would tender their personal fortunes, moreover without any expectation of return within a reasonable time frame.

Finally, in 1781, Haym Salomon's role in history was assured. General Washington planned to join his forces with the French to defeat the British, but he needed at least twenty thousand dollars to finance this great effort. After meeting in New York, Washington and Morris agreed that there was only one man capable of raising such a sum – millions in today's dollars. Who did they turn to? Our hero, Haym Salomon!

General Washington sent an emissary to Philadelphia to seek out Haym Salomon. As the story goes, the messenger arrived during the Jewish High Holidays and knocked on the door of the synagogue, asking for our hero. Upon hearing of Washington's dilemma, Haym interrupted the service and pleaded to his fellow congregants to support Washington's troops. "Our very freedom and liberty are at stake here. We must support the general and his troops!"

History records that Haym Salomon raised more than the twenty thousand dollars needed by Washington. He saved the day for the general and the fledgling nation. With money in hand, Washington inflicted on the British at Yorktown (with the help of the French navy, which confronted the British fleet in New York) the greatest military defeat they had suffered in the colonies. General Charles Cornwallis lost to General Washington, and the British surrendered their arms. An amazing victory for the Americans. They had defeated the better-established British army!

The city of Philadelphia erupted with joy, celebrating the news of the American triumph. How do you think our hero Haym Salomon felt? Certainly he reflected on the fact that he had played such an important role in this great victory. But, it should be noted in fact, many other Jews had also contributed to the American revolutionary cause, including Mordecai Sheftall of Georgia, Georgia governor David Emanuel, and Manuel Noah of North Carolina, to name a few.

No one surpassed Haym Salomon's contributions. He was the epitome of financial support, upon which Washington and Morris leaned in time of need. In 1941, Franklin Roosevelt referred to Salomon and Morris thusly: "Their genius in finance and fiscal affairs and unselfish devotion to the cause of liberty made their support of utmost importance when the struggling colonies were fighting against such heavy odds."[6]

Haym continued his charitable work in his later years, helping to build a new house of worship for his synagogue, Congregation Mikveh Israel, in Philadelphia. He pledged to underwrite 75 percent of the total cost himself!

January 6, 1785, marked the passing of Haym Salomon – a hero of the Revolutionary War who had never worn a military uniform. He had given so much to others that, in death, he could not provide for his family. His estate consisted for the most part of continental currency, which had diminished in value, and his family was now totally bankrupt. He had been one of the richest men in the colonies, but did not live to see the birth of his only son, Haym – named after him. He also would never live to see his beloved wife again, nor would he be able to experience the love and joy of his family together.

Haym's family was never repaid by all the debtors to whom he had loaned money. The federal government never provided any aid to his widow. Even Robert Morris did not reinforce Rachel's claims for compensation, though he could have done so.

But Haym Salomon nevertheless left a legacy that many more famous men would envy. He provided funds that kept the struggling United States alive, enabling it to win its independence from Britain.

A statue of Haym Salomon, George Washington, and Robert

---

6 Renee Critcher Lyons, *Foreign-Born American Patriots: Sixteen Volunteer Leaders in the Revolutionary War* (London: McFarland, 2014), 40.

Morris honors those heroes in Chicago, and another statue of Haym can be found in Los Angeles. A US postage stamp, issued in 1975, reads, "Businessman and broker Haym Salomon was responsible for raising most of the money needed to finance the American Revolution and later to save the nation from collapse."[7]

Why isn't there a monument to Haym Solomon in Washington, DC, where our hero's name is barely mentioned? Why not a lasting tribute to our hero? What could be more appropriate for an American patriot who loved his adopted country so much that he devoted his life and fortune to help guarantee its survival? Haym Salomon gave his all to save his country; a lasting reminder of his legacy would remind future generations that freedom is not free, and that sacrifices and hardships sometimes need to be made and endured to ensure the continuity of our way of life.

Sons of Liberty (1939), a movie about Haym Salomon starring Claude Raines, won an Academy Award for Best Short Subject. The last scene in the movie depicts our hero on his deathbed, stricken with tuberculosis. In attendance are his wife Rachel, his rabbi, and the rest of his family. Haym pulls himself up in his bed, looks at the assembled, and then pronounces for all to hear, "We hold these truths to be self-evident, that all men are created equal, that they are endowed by their creator with certain unalienable rights, that among these are life, liberty, and the pursuit of happiness." He then settles back and passes on, a great American hero. Like Thomas Jefferson, whose words in the Declaration of Independence he had quoted, Haym believed that liberty and freedom were the most important of a man's possessions. He died penniless and in debt.

---

7   Ibid.

4. Uriah Phillips Levy

||||||||||||||||||||||||||||||||||||||||||||||||||||||||

Uriah Phillips Levy was an early American military hero who rose to the rank of commodore in the US Navy (equivalent to today's rank of rear admiral), and was also the first legendary Jewish naval leader.

Uriah was born in Philadelphia, Pennsylvania, on April 22, 1792, sixteen years after the Declaration of Independence. He was of Hispanic origin, descended from Sephardic Jews who had left Spain to avoid the Inquisition of 1492. As a young boy, Uriah was quick-tempered and very proud, traits that would define him his entire life. He was also heavily influenced in his youth by his maternal grandfather, Jonas Phillips – an ardent patriot, a soldier in the Revolution, and a religious Jew who served as president of the Mikveh Israel synagogue in Philadelphia. Uriah also came to admire one of his grandfather's idols, Thomas Jefferson.

At the early age of ten, Uriah unexpectedly decided to sign up as an apprentice seaman aboard the merchant ship *New Jerusalem* (of all names!). He later came home for his bar mitzvah, at thirteen, but left again afterward to return to the sea as an apprentice to a Mr. John Coulter. He was still only thirteen years old! Then, having served four years in his apprenticeship, he became a seaman in 1806 on the schooner *Rittenhouse*. From there, Uriah attended navigation school for two years before sailing again in 1809 on one of two different sister ships as second mate; he was now only sixteen years old.

At age seventeen, after a two-year apprenticeship, he became captain and third owner of a schooner called *George Washington*; then, at nineteen, a ship owner in full – an amazing feat for such a young man in the early days of the United States.

During the War of 1812, Uriah became an acting lieutenant aboard the *Argus* before it was captured by the British. The *Argus* arrived at Lorient June 12, 1812, and then cruised off the British coast, making many important enemy captures before being captured herself. Uriah was a valuable prize for the British, and remained incarcerated in Dartmoor Prison, in England, for eighteen months, until after the war's end.

Uriah then became sailing master on the *Franklin* in 1816, at age twenty-five. Here he had his first encounter with antisemitism; challenged by a drunken officer, Uriah retaliated and was provoked by the officer into a duel. Uriah initially refused, but eventually relented, and he subsequently fought and killed the officer. Strangely, he was indicted by a grand jury but was found not guilty.

In 1819, at the age of twenty-seven, our hero was given a commission as third lieutenant aboard the *United States*. Unbelievably, Uriah – proud as ever – got into another altercation with the ship's lieutenant. Uriah was very sure that he was again being victimized as a Jew and was singled out by this antisemitic lieutenant. The result? Uriah was court-martialed and dismissed from the navy. But two years later, President James Monroe reversed his sentence on the advice of Secretary of the Navy Smith Thompson. Uriah was given command of the *Revenge*, a schooner of 158 guns – at the age of only twenty-nine years!

Another incident, in 1825, further defines our hero. While acting as second lieutenant on the *Cyane*, he saved the life of an American who had been forced to serve in the Brazilian navy. Remarkably, when Dom Pedro, the emperor of Brazil, heard of this, he offered Uriah the rank of captain in the Brazilian navy. Uriah's responded that he would rather serve as a cabin boy in the US Navy than an admiral for any other country in the world.[8]

The years following this incident saw Uriah enter the real estate business in New York City, since he was not getting assignments from the US Navy. Thus, he went into private business and became very

---

8   Irving Litvag, *Commodore Levy: A Novel of Early America in the Age of Sail* (Lubbock, TX: Texas Tech University Press, 2014).

affluent, making astute purchases during the growing New York City real estate boom. Uriah commissioned a statue of Thomas Jefferson from the sculptor Pierre-Jean David d'Angers in 1832. In 1834 Uriah donated the statue to the American people, though Congress did not accept it until 1874 (forty years later)!

In 1835, now back in the navy, and after twenty years as a lieutenant, Uriah was promoted to commander and assigned to the ship *Vandalia*. He was now intent on doing away with the lash and wanted new rules and regulations for sailor conduct and discipline. He began petitioning to end the practice of flogging.

These reform ideas were not well received at all, and, wouldn't you know it, Uriah was court-martialed again in 1842, at the age of fifty. He was dismissed from the navy, and once again our commodore sincerely believed he was a victim of more antisemitism. But once again, the president at the time, John Tyler, reversed the court's verdict. Then, to Commander Levy's total amazement, he received a promotion to captain. Captain, after a court-martial? What was going on in the navy?

Around this time, Senator John Hale of New Hampshire joined Uriah in protesting the practice of flogging in the navy. In 1850 Congress finally limited the use of the lash by attaching an anti-flogging rider to the Naval Appropriations Bill. Our hero had finally done something significant for the US Navy and its enlisted sailors. The US Navy was the first to abolish corporal punishment.

In 1855, Uriah was rebuked by the naval board, for no good cause, when he requested a new commission. Undeterred, Uriah hired noted attorney Benjamin Butler to petition Congress on his behalf. Yet again, fate shined on our hero: in 1858, Congress restored him to active duty. Four months later, Captain Levy took command of the sloop-of-war *Macedonian* in the Mediterranean Sea. He then became a flag officer in 1860 and was referred to as Commodore Levy. (Congress only established the rank of commodore in the navy in 1862; prior to that, commodore was an unofficial earned title of respect.) He had finally achieved his dream.

With the start of the Civil War, Commodore Levy offered his military services and his entire fortune to save the Union.[9] President Abraham Lincoln was so impressed that he installed Levy on the Court Martial Board in Washington (despite Levy's court-martials and various run-ins with authority figures).

Commodore Levy died on March 26, 1862, at seventy years of age. He received full military honors at his funeral, which included a traditional Jewish ceremony as well. In World War II, the naval destroyer escort USS *Levy*, named in our hero's honor, hosted the surrender ceremonies of the Japanese navy. In addition, the Jewish chapel at the US naval base in Norfolk, Virginia, was dedicated in his name in 1959, and the Jewish chapel at the United States Naval Academy in Annapolis, Maryland, was dedicated in his name in 2005. (Our hero was a religious man and was the first president of the Washington Hebrew Congregation in Washington, DC).

Uriah Levy was a pugnacious, determined, eccentric man, who believed in the righteousness of his causes. Although he became a very wealthy businessman, he never forgot the ideal of religious liberty embraced by Thomas Jefferson. He was a dedicated admirer of Jefferson, and had the opportunity and the means to buy Monticello during his lifetime. He did so, and restored the decaying residence to its original beauty and splendor for future generations.

He said many times, "I consider Thomas Jefferson to be one of the greatest men in history.... He serves as an inspiration to millions of Americans. He did much to mold our republic in a form in which a man's religion does not make him ineligible for political or governmental life."[10]

Uriah Levy lived his life on his own terms. He stood up to antisemitism and to his own government, and he achieved greatness while doing so. Commodore Levy, by his great dedication to the American

---

9   Shades of Haym Salomon, who loaned his entire fortune to the US government and the leading politicians of the day!

10   Quoted in Kurt F. Stone, *The Jews of Capitol Hill: A Compendium of Jewish Congressional Members* (New York: Scarecrow Press, 2010), 69.

way of life and his service to his country, was remembered with a statue on December 30, 2011, at Congregation Mikveh Israel in Philadelphia. In attendance were many distinguished scholars and naval commanders, including former Secretary of the Navy John Lehman and Rear Admiral Herman Shelanski; both were speakers at the event. Many of the speakers focused on the important role Commodore Levy played in setting the stage for all future Jewish Americans to serve with distinction in the US armed forces.

At the top of the statue, a bronze plaque displays the following quote from Commodore Levy: "I am an American, a sailor, and a Jew."

Rest in peace, our hero Commodore Levy.

Part 3
||||||||||||||

AMAZING JEWISH HEROES
OF THE HOLOCAUST

5. Felix Zandman
||||||||||||||||||||||||||||||||||||||||||||||

Have you ever been in a really darkened room – pitch black – with no switch to turn on the light? Or been locked in a dark room and unable to escape? Worse, imagine being placed in a hole in the ground four feet deep, five and a half by five feet, with three of your relatives and friends but without running water, electricity, toilet facilities, and heat or air conditioning. How long do you think any human being – let alone four – could endure and function, could live anything like a normal life, under such conditions? If you said a day or two, a week or two, even a month or two, you would still not even be close to what our hero Felix (Feivel) Zandman endured in 1943 with his relatives. How did he do it? How did they survive? What motivated these people to endure these conditions, winter and summer, through hot days and sub-zero temperatures?

Felix was born in 1927 in Grodno, Poland (today Belarus). His family on his mother's side, the Freydoviczes, were wealthy industrialists. His father, Aaron Zandman, had married into this family and become a junior partner in the business. Felix's paternal grandfather was an Orthodox Jew who taught Felix to pray and to lay tefillin. Felix's younger years were filled with discussions of the Bible, the Talmud, and Zionism – the Zandmans believed in the founding of a Jewish homeland. His grandmother, Rifka, was the daughter of a famous holy man, the Kelmer Maggid. His sermons, in which he implored well-to-do Jews to give to the poor and provide jobs for those less fortunate, were legendary. Felix was known to be the Maggid's great-grandson, and was honored in the synagogue for this lineage. Both families influenced Felix's thinking: the Zandmans, where talk always revolved around religion and politics, and the Freydoviczes, where discussions centered on business and practical affairs. He was deeply loved by both families and returned that love in good measure.

But the relative who had the greatest impact on Felix throughout his entire life was his Grandma Tema Freydovicz. Felix's maternal grandmother taught him that everything in life of a material nature – one's house, store, or clothes – can be taken away, but no one can take away the knowledge one learns. She always took Felix with her when she visited hospitals, old age homes, and orphanages, and instilled in him the calling of helping the less fortunate. "We have a great deal. But the only things we own are the things we give away. That's all we really have. If you help a person, if you give of yourself – that no one can ever take away from you."[11] That was Tema's mantra.

Jews had lived in the environs of the city of Grodno, Poland, since the late 1300s, when they were granted a charter by Grand Duke Vitold of Lithuania. Grodno had proved an attractive place for Jews, and they had transformed the community into a commercial and religious center. Of the total population of fifty thousand, more than half of Grodno's inhabitants (thirty thousand people) were Jewish. But although intercommunal relations were generally peaceful, antisemitism still lurked under the surface. Felix, who lived near a Catholic church, had to run for his life as gangs of Catholic Polish boys pursued him. Even in the public schools, which were government-sponsored, there was blatant prejudice; only two or three Jewish students were admitted into each class. Jews who wanted to attend a university in Poland were not considered qualified, even though their level of learning was often superior to that of their Polish counterparts.

At a young age, Felix decided to become an engineer. Meeting the challenge of solving difficult problems gave him great satisfaction. He attended a local Tarbut school, part of a secular Zionist educational network in which Hebrew was the language of instruction. At twelve

---

11 These quotations and all those that follow in this chapter are from Felix Zandman's autobiography, *Never the Last Journey*, written with David Chanoff (New York: Schocken, 1995), unless otherwise noted.

years old, Felix was impressed with the idea of a Jewish state, despite his father's objections (his father supported a unified state with Arabs as equal participants). He loved the idea of settling in Eretz Israel and living in a kibbutz, even though in those days the Jewish Yishuv in Palestine was an economically depressed community, positively primitive by European standards, and had a precarious future. Many Jews embraced Zionism at this time, in the late 1930s, but most were not motivated enough to leave their friends, families, and businesses.

In Poland, at the same time, there was word of worsening conditions for Jews in Germany. The Yiddish newspapers chronicled serious incidents involving Jews there, but life continued as usual despite the danger that seemed to be right around the corner. And then Germany began its invasion of Poland. When France and Great Britain declared war on Germany everyone thought Germany would be defeated very soon. Unfortunately, the opposite occurred – Germany invaded Poland successfully, and the Polish army could not stop them. Even after Russia entered Poland and pacified Grodno and the other towns under its control, the Jews were concerned. At first, the Russians gave Jews total equality in their communist society, which enraged many Catholic Poles. Soon after, these policies changed and Jews again became refugees in their own homeland. The Russians began closing down Jewish schools and prohibited the teaching of Zionism; they even opposed anyone who was openly a Zionist – a believer in a Jewish homeland. People began to be displaced from their homes. Grandma Tema confided in Felix that she wanted to be rid of both the Russians and the Germans. "What do you want, Grandma?" Felix asked. Her answer: "*Ich will Roosevelt*" (I want Roosevelt) – she prayed for the Americans to come to their rescue.

Then it happened. On June 22, 1941, Germany again crossed the border into Poland. War had begun between Russia and Germany. Felix's grandparents' town, Slonim, was attacked while Felix was visiting them, and the town was soon in flames. They all tried escaping, but it was too late. The next day, they observed Germans in gray uniforms rounding up Jewish men. But these were not ordinary German soldiers – they were the *Einsatzgruppen*, the SS units whose specialty was murdering Jews. Felix and his grandparents finally managed to escape to Grodno to join the rest of the family, but they soon learned that there too German soldiers were rounding up Jews and taking them in truckloads to be shot. The family was terrified. What to do? Jews were soon required to sew yellow stars on their coats, over their hearts, and were ordered to walk in the street instead of on the sidewalks. They were also obliged to doff their hats to German soldiers.

Felix's world quickly became one of spiritual degradation thanks to the antisemitic barbarism he experienced. The humiliation haunted Felix, and he feared for his family's lives. Pogroms were on everyone's minds. The Germans finally decreed that all Jews must live in assigned areas, or ghettos. Anyone found outside the perimeter of the ghetto would be shot.

The Zandman family managed to survive in the Grodno ghetto until 1942, but not without cost. One day, Felix, seeing a patrol approaching him, walked the other way. The Germans noticed this and ran after him. They caught him and beat him with their rifle butts, and Felix feared for his life. The Germans finally tired of their assault and left him there on the ground. Fortunately, passersby helped Felix stand and walk, and he made it home. There, where they had already heard of his resistance, he was treated like a hero.

Another incident shook Felix to his core. One day, a crowd gathered near Felix's front door. Watching through the window, he noticed among them Lena Prenska, a family friend, along with the Jewish police chief and the principal of his Tarbut school, Dr. Braver. The German commandant, Wiese, known as "the angel of death" and dressed in black, was there giving orders.[12] Soon, the three victims were led to where three nooses hung from a building. They were forced to stand on a wooden bench under the nooses. Soon, with the nooses firmly in

---

12 In Simon Wiesenthal's memoirs, *The Murderers Among Us: The Simon Wiesenthal Memoirs*, ed. Joseph Wechsberg (New York: McGraw-Hill, 1967), the famed Nazi hunter leaves no stone unturned in pursuing Commandant Kurt Wiese for his war crimes. In chapter 6 of the present book, that story unfolds and confirms that truth is stranger than fiction.

place, all three were dead, hanging like paper dolls! Lena, a beautiful young girl, had been caught hiding outside the ghetto with the others. This was to be a lesson to all the Jews in the ghetto from their evil Nazi captors.

Jews were being removed from the ghetto and transported somewhere, but no one knew where. Rumors abounded that they were being gassed and burned, but no one believed these stories – "How could that be?" they wondered. Gas chambers and ovens? A world of fantasy. It couldn't be true.

On November 1, 1942, they were told the ghetto was closing – the deportations were starting! The Zandmans were transported, along with most of the rest of the ghetto, to a labor camp. There, Felix began working, mixing cement and carrying it to bricklayers. He was surviving and bringing home food he bought from his fellow Polish workers. But this arrangement was short-lived: the Germans began systematically moving the Jews to Kielbasin – a harsh labor camp with a terrible reputation. Stories were told of hangings and executions there, terrifying Felix and his family again. What would become of them? His family – now just his father and mother– felt they were doomed, but Felix's instincts were to get out, to escape. He finally did exactly this, escaping back to Grodno by jumping off a potato wagon and hiding in a ditch.

In Grodno, some of Felix's extended family, including Grandma Tema, had not yet been deported. But almost thirty thousand Jews had vanished from Grodno as if they had never existed. Survival was on everyone's mind. One night, yet again, the area was surrounded by German soldiers who were to "clean out" the ghetto of Jews. Felix's family created an escape hatch to a hiding place above the kitchen. Only eight people could fit inside, while lying flat. Who would be chosen? The family decided that the young ones – the brothers and sisters and cousins, including Felix – would survive in the hiding place.

Screams, barking dogs, and gunshots were soon heard. People were being herded into transports yet again. Days passed, and the family remained hidden under terrible conditions, squeezed together, with little air. They were in pain; their anguish was unbearable. Felix finally left, unable to bear his family's suffering any longer. He had to go into hiding somewhere else, but where? Friends he met, who had also managed to escape the transports, told him of a house in the woods where the Puchalski family lived. They had been caretakers of his Freydovicz grandparents' dachas for many years. But before he could get to the Puchalskis, Felix first needed to get away from the ghetto.

On his way, Felix ran into a Polish woman from whom he had bought half a bottle of vodka days before. He begged her to hide him. "Just for today, and then I'll leave," Felix pleaded. She refused, telling him to go back to the ghetto.

Felix, just fifteen, was very concerned about his plight. Where to go? What to do? The few thousand Jews left were being rounded up, women and children first.

He finally found the house of the Zandmans' former nanny, where he found refuge. Felix was directed to the stable to sleep with the cow and in the morning, after being kicked by the cow, he was brought porridge by his hostess. After two days in the stable, Felix felt he had to move on, and he thought again about the Puchalskis. Where else could he go?

He trekked through the Losossna woods outside Grodno, arrived at the Puchalskis' house, and knocked on the door. Janova Puchalski was a big-boned, robust woman, whose broad face lit up with surprise when she saw Felix. She took him in her arms and kissed him! With that, Felix boldly said, "Pani Janova, can you let me stay for the night? Just one night, and then I'll go." Janova then responded, "Felix, you'll go nowhere!"

Felix did not know then that Janova, when she was pregnant with her second daughter, Sabina, had been thrown out of her own house by her drunken husband. She had no money and nowhere to go. She finally came to Grodno, and Grandma Tema's house, where she was taken in and given a place to live. Grandma Tema even arranged for her to have her baby delivered in Grodno's Jewish hospital. Felix, when he heard this story, was not surprised; Grandma Tema had performed thousands of good deeds for the community. Janova continued, "So you see, you are a gift to me from God. I will not let you perish, Felix. If you perish, we will all perish. You will not go anyplace. We will take care of you!"

Felix had found refuge, but he worried about his relatives. One evening, while he was lying in bed in his small bedroom, the door flew open and someone jumped into bed with him. Unbelievably, it was his Uncle Sender! His story, as he told it to Felix, was equally shocking.

He had been at work at a construction site, a hotel in the town. Suddenly, his group had been surrounded by German soldiers and marched back to the ghetto. Nearing the entrance gate, Sender noticed two groups forming – some on the left, and the others on the right. He surmised the group on the right was safe, so he eased toward that side. He was also strong and fit, and was sure he would be selected to live, not die. But, as fate would have it, he was pushed to the left.

Not to be denied, he moved quickly to the group on the right. Here he was noticed by the evil commandant, Wiese, who grabbed him by the collar. "Turn around and walk," he said. Fateful words, because Sender knew that meant a bullet in the head!

Uncle Sender took off, running down the street with all the speed he could muster. By the time Wiese finally readied his machine gun and shot a volley of bullets, Sender had hidden himself in a narrow alley. A Jewish policeman saw him and warned him of his pursuers. "Get away from here!" he yelled.

Sender then found an apartment building where a friend, Bass, lived. Sender got him to find his brother, Kushka, who was also a friend of Sender's and who brought him a five-ruble gold piece and told him about the Puchalski family, where he could hide "for a day or two." Sender also learned that the remaining women and children had been taken away, including his wife Sarah and their two babies. Sender slipped away from the ghetto. In a state of shock, nearly delirious from the loss haunting him, he found the Puchalskis' house.

Before long, four other friends had joined them at the Puchalski home, for a total of six survivors. A potato cellar behind the house was their refuge temporarily, but it posed many risks. This became a problem for all to consider seriously, because if it were suspected that Jews were hiding at the house, everyone there would be executed, including the Puchalski family!

So Sender devised a plan: they would dig a small cellar under the second bedroom. They had to dig with caution, because removing the dirt could alert a passerby or, worse, a soldier. Their hiding place was a hole five feet wide, five and a half feet long, and four feet deep! Felix thought it looked like a grave. Six people could get down there, and then live there? A channel for air was dug out to the yard, where it was hidden by the garden. The Puchalskis also moved their doghouse to that side of the house – this way, smells from the hole might appear to be from the dog. Fresh straw was spread on the floor, and the hole was ready for the six survivors. Three people could lie on the floor, and two others could sit between them. The last person could sit on the small tin can that served as the toilet! For light they relied on a tiny oil lamp.

Outside, the temperature was below zero; inside, it was hot and humid, blacker than night. Sender was next to his friend Bass and Bass's wife. Soon loud snoring pierced the stillness, and everyone realized Sender's friend the policeman Zamosczanki and his wife must leave. It was too dangerous. Finally, the remaining Jews numbered four: Felix, Sender, and Mottl and Goldie Bass. Two men, an adolescent, and a woman – how were they going to survive? Rules would have to be made, in order to "live civilized," Sender proclaimed. There would be no sex for Mottl and Goldie, for starters. Second, everyone would change places every two hours; everyone would share the same conditions. Finally, food would be shared equally. Once or twice a day, Janova handed down the meal, which they then ate in the darkness. Why? Because the smell of burning oil from their small lamp made the food unpleasant to eat! At the same time, the waste bucket was taken up to be emptied.

So Felix lived in a nocturnal world, where worms were constant companions and fleas plagued the four as well – not to mention the lice, which Felix learned to pop between his nails. Not being able to launder their clothes became a problem, so delousing by hand became something of a sport in the sparse lamplight – lice seemed to be everywhere. Washing one's body could only be done every few months, up in the house, using a wooden tub Janova filled with hot water. They had to finish quickly while the Puchalski children kept watch outside. What a way to live! But they never gave up on their thirst for life.

Once, Janova's thudding foot alerted them to danger. Germans were in the house! Would they be discovered? All kept still while the Puchalskis' dog, Muska, barked at the Germans' dog. But the moment passed. Later, Janova divulged that she had scattered pepper to foil the German dog's sense of smell.

Still those four – ragged and filthy – never despaired. In the house above them, Janova also never lost her optimism or resourcefulness. Knowing that buying food for an extra four people could alert the authorities, she started a rumor that she was speculating in food. Bass gave her a gold piece every month or so, which allowed her to buy beef or lamb, providing a feast that day for Felix and his companions.

Months passed. Felix wondered in the darkness, *Will we be alive in another hour, another minute?* This constant anxiety, the worry that each strange sound could signal their doom, permeated their existence in that hole.

Felix also dreamed of vengeance and wanted to kill the Germans for what they had done to his mother and father. Bass had told him of Jewish resistance groups that had formed, but no action had yet been taken, because the rabbis and community leaders had recommended patience. They would survive.

Felix and Sender yearned many times to leave their hole. Each time, Sender would resist the urge, saying, "Sheer nonsense." The fact was that they were a thousand miles behind German lines, where every Jew was being murdered. Period.

Eretz Israel, too, was on their minds. Felix remembered what some ghetto inhabitants had said when they were being led to the trucks: "Don't forget Israel, you who are left alive! Fight for Israel! *Fargess nisht*

Yisroel! (Forget not Israel!)" Their fate had been sealed, their last and only testament delivered.

So Felix whiled away the hours and days thinking; thinking about the Puchalskis, heroes to him and his companions – he would reward them someday; he also thought about sex (he was a sixteen-year-old, with a sixteen-year-old's hormones); and he thought about music, as he recalled his violin and his days of playing Mozart and Beethoven. He read books of Russian poems and memorized them for the hours of dark when the light was out.

Sender, concerned about Felix, assumed a guardian's role. Sender was a teacher, and one of his interests, which Felix happened to share, was mathematics. Day after day Sender taught Felix all aspects of algebra and geometry, questioning and challenging him until he understood. In the darkness, Felix memorized mathematical equations and solved geometry and algebra exercises. Knowledge was a passion for Felix; he and Sender discussed many subjects, including Polish history.

The progression of the Jewish holidays was an enigma without a calendar. Figuring out when the Passover, Yom Kippur, and Rosh Hashanah holidays would fall was Bass's forte. He would calculate in his head the days that had passed, and would predict the start of a holiday. "Tomorrow is Pesach – no bread to be eaten," he would say. Thus the holidays were observed in their dark home!

All these guidelines helped to sustain the four, but above all, their survival was based on Sender's rules: no sex, no quarrels, and equal food. These rules kept them in tune with everyday, normal living, like the reason the Ten Commandments were created by God – to guide Jews in their everyday life.

One day, they heard news that the Germans were retreating, bringing the Russians closer to Grodno. They even welcomed a new guest, Esther Heidemark, whose husband had supplied Sender with a dental tool to extract an infected wisdom tooth. She knew of their secret hideout and joined them after her husband's arrest.

More good news came in June 1944 – the Americans had invaded Europe at Normandy! They also learned that town after town was being liberated by the Soviets, and that they were getting closer and closer to Grodno. Then, one day, they heard muffled German speech outside and the noise of an automobile. Had they been discovered after all? Tremors vibrated through the house, but as evening fell, they subsided. Sender carefully left their hideout and found that the Germans were in full retreat in that area. But the next day brought more rifle shots, as well as machine-gun fire. What was happening? Again, all went quiet. The next day, July 14, they were told that the Grodno railroad station had been torched by the retreating German army. The following day, there was a digging sound close by them, surprising them, but again nothing came of it. On Sunday, July 16, they heard loud noises all around the house. Motorcycle engines screamed overhead, soldiers shouted in German, "*Macht schnell!*" (Hurry up!). Then Janova, shouting: "Have to leave the fighting here, must get out!" Then silence again. Only goats could be heard, shuffling across the floorboards above.

What was happening? The group of five now sat in the sweltering heat with very little to eat and a waste bucket, unemptied for two days, stinking terribly. They all thought, *We're dead. The Germans will find us now, for sure!*

Sender pleaded with Felix, who desperately wanted to leave. Felix, who had been brave throughout the seventeen-month trial, was crying. Sender quieted him again, not wanting him to leave. "Stay here – you cannot go!"

To make matters worse, Germans occupied the house above and noticed the smell of the waste! Nothing happened, however, and the Germans soon went to sleep. What to do now? Sender went up into the house to survey the scene around them. A German was sleeping on a sofa in the main room, just eight or nine feet from their trap door! Sender returned, and a decision was made: to escape the next night!

They made their plans by finalizing their stories and organizing their passports. If they were caught by Germans, they would say they were running from Bolsheviks and had survived in a shelter until it was destroyed by artillery the previous night.

Finally the time came to leave their hole, after seventeen long months! In spite of the German sleeping on the couch, they each climbed quietly out the trap door, one by one. They then slipped out the bedroom window, and were immediately overwhelmed by the fresh air and the strong smell of pine. For the very first time in almost a year and a half, they were above ground and alive!

Twenty yards from the house, however, they suddenly heard a scream of "Halt!" A German soldier came over to them, weapon in hand, demanding to know who they were and where they came from. After seventeen months living in a filthy, lice-infested pit, barely surviving, they now faced mortal danger – after only a few minutes of "freedom." They stood before this soldier, rail-thin, in their tattered, filthy clothing. They said they were fleeing a nearby village ahead of the Russian invasion. After looking them up and down, the soldier let them go. Hearts racing, they fled into the forest. They had come within a heartbeat of being shot to death, right on the spot, after their hellish ordeal in hiding!

They soon made their way to the village of Losossna, rested, and continued on to Bialystok.

Free at last, Felix began to think about his future. He thought of going to Eretz Israel as a free man. He even started collecting guns for a mission to supply arms to Palestine. Sender stepped in again and convinced Felix that his destiny was to go to university, for at least a year. Felix finally agreed and started his studies at the Danzig Polytechnicum. This proved to be a fateful move. Soon afterward, he was invited to Paris for a conference of Polish Jewish students. Recognizing the plight of Polish Jews, a French union of Jewish students had arranged visas for sixty Polish Jewish students; Felix signed his visa with the others, including Uncle Sender, with no intention of ever returning to Poland.

Felix excelled in university – after just three years he had earned three certificates, or degrees, in engineering, physics, and applied mechanics. He was only twenty-two years old. Where would he go now? He had long desired to go to Eretz Israel, but a friend from Grodno, Joseph Weiss, helped him acknowledge his responsibilities as a survivor. Felix had pleaded, "It's my duty – I have to go." But Weiss was firm, saying, "Felix, you're the last one from your family, you're the seed – everyone is dead, all those children, everyone. You are the only survivor; you can't do it to the memory of your family. The seed of Zandman has to create a family – you cannot go to Eretz Israel and be killed."

In France, Felix met and married a girl, Ruth, whose father was a cantor. Felix yearned for a family, although Ruth's parents were not happy with their daughter's marriage to this refugee, an alien in their country, no less (in fact the marriage ultimately broke up in 1974). Felix and Ruth settled down, Ruth finding a job and Felix working for a generator manufacturer. A few months later, Felix was awarded a grant sponsoring him to study for a doctorate at St. Cyr, a Sorbonne-affiliated laboratory.

At St. Cyr Laboratories, Felix was eager to begin his life's work. He took an interest in photoelasticity and began experimenting with bonding plastic to various surfaces, especially metals. These plastics could then be analyzed to help engineers measure stress on everything from airplane wings, missiles, and engines to bridges and skyscrapers. His research was published, and the book was acquired by many libraries worldwide.

Soon thereafter, Felix and his wife at last toured Israel; when he returned he began working as a laboratory engineer at SNECMA, a government-owned airplane engine manufacturer. Here he was able to test his theories on actual airplane wings, improving the manufacturing process with measuring devices he developed. Then, to his surprise, he found himself working with German engineers on a new engine design. This turned out to be the engine for the Mystère jets destined for Israel. He had observed that they were being developed for low-level flight, and had questioned the purpose of the design. When he found out that the Dead Sea was the intended region of operation, he knew his suspicions had been correct.

Felix, now aware his PhotoStress technology was valid, began procuring patents on his work. He quickly received great interest, but SNECMA, his employer, did not want to pursue that line of work as a business. Felix, disappointed, then left SNECMA to form a joint venture called Scientific Instruments. Now he was on his own, with an office and a secretary. Even though he had never before felt an entrepreneurial impulse, he now had a clear path to his scientific goals.

Felix had come a long way since his ordeal in Grodno, and now American industry called. A headhunter named Marc Wood called, seeking French scientists to go to America. This took Felix to New York for ten days, where he became a consultant under contract. After settling his affairs in France, Felix decided to remain in America and began publishing papers in his field of specialty – photoelastic coatings. This brought him great interest from many companies, including the Budd Company of Philadelphia, a giant manufacturer of railroad cars. They wanted new ideas to improve their electrical measuring devices, and they thought Felix's PhotoStress concept would work for them. After a demonstration of Felix's concept to the head of Budd's measuring device division, called Tatnall Measuring Systems, Felix was hired as director of their research and PhotoStress departments. Felix did not yet speak English, so in his new capacity he began learning thirty words a day – nine hundred words a month. He did so because he would be expected to lecture, and his English needed to be perfected. Although he was ashamed of his French-Polish-Yiddish accent, he was informed by his boss, Frank Tatnall, "Everyone loves you, Felix – okay? Secondly, never lose your accent!"

Felix's reputation soon grew all over the United States, but he was challenged on his PhotoStress theory. At a national conference in Washington, he proved to all the scientists, including those from MIT and UCLA, that his idea was practically faultless.

He also visited his uncle Jake Slaner in Oklahoma, who had settled in a small town there many years before and opened a store that became very successful. They talked about the "old country" for many hours, even recalling Grandma Tema, who had envied Jake's success when he had visited Poland many years before. Jake also encouraged Felix to stay close to his own son, Alfred, for one day, he was sure, Alfred would be Felix's business partner.

Felix was succeeding professionally in the United States, and socially as well, joining and being active in a philanthropy group for Israel's equivalent of MIT, the Technion, as well as many Jewish organizations. But emotionally, the scars from his days in Grodno haunted him. He couldn't talk about the past; he felt no one who had not lived through it would understand – how could they?

While working at Budd, Felix began thinking of trying to create a new type of resistor, one that would be impervious to changes in temperature and thus many times better than conventional resistors. Inspired in part by his knowledge of bondings associated with PhotoStress technology, Felix came up with the idea of bonding metal to a rigid substrate, and thus creating a resistor that would not be impacted by temperature fluctuations. Such a resistor would be ideal for use in instrumentation, aircraft, and other products and systems that require ultra-high precision and reliability. When Budd declined to fund his project, Felix decided to go into business for himself.

After seeking out his cousin Alfred Slaner, he left Budd. Alfred had agreed to loan Felix five thousand dollars to start his business. He named his new company Vishay, after the tiny Lithuanian village where Grandma Tema and Jake Slaner, Alfred's father, had been born. The name evoked powerful memories of those who had perished in the Holocaust – Vishay's Jews had been wiped off the face of the earth. Felix founded his company in 1962.

After six months of work, Felix and his associates at Vishay succeeded at producing the resistor he had dreamed of: the Bulk Metal foil resistor. It steadily gained acceptance and became widely used in commercial aircraft, jet fighters, NASA spacecraft, precision instrumentation, computers, and more. Vishay became a very successful company and the world's leading manufacturer of foil resistors, PhotoStress products, and strain gages.

After Vishay experienced two decades of organic growth, Felix decided to expand the company through acquisitions. The acquisitions of Dale Electronics (USA), Draloric Electronic (Germany), Sfernice (France), Sprague Electric (USA), and others produced dramatic sales growth. By 1992 Vishay had become a billion-dollar company. In 1993, *Fortune* magazine's issue on the nation's largest industrial corporations included Vishay among the Top 500. The list included GE, Intel, and Motorola. Our hero Felix had come full circle. He said at that moment: "Not so bad for a company named after a vanished Jewish shtetl."

Felix never lost his love for Israel. He built factories there. This advanced his participation in Israel's quest for excellence in weaponry – in 1971, he was asked by General Israel Tal, the Israel Defense Force's greatest tank commander, to help develop a tank cannon that would not be affected by the sun's heat in the desert. Missing a target by as little as a yard would negate the tank's effectiveness. So what did Felix do? He developed a thermal sleeve that deflected heat by distributing it, increasing the precision of the cannon, which proved invaluable in the 1982 Lebanon war.

Vishay built several plants in Israel – in Holon, Dimona, Be'er Sheva, and Migdal Ha'Emek – and created many thousands of jobs.

During one of Felix's trips to Israel, he visited Yad Vashem, the Holocaust memorial in Jerusalem. He had never been there; the thought had made him very uncomfortable. Finally, in 1986 with his second wife, Ruta, he decided to participate in the Yom HaShoah (Holocaust Remembrance Day) ceremony there.

As he approached the site, his feelings overwhelmed him. He could not even open the door to the memorial hall, where the names of the dead and the burning memorial candles were located. He and his wife and daughter left – he was not ready to come to terms with his past.

A year later, in 1987, he found out that Yad Vashem was bestowing the honor of "Righteous Among the Nations" upon those who had saved Jewish lives during the Holocaust. The Puchalski family had been nominated, and after a year of investigation it was decided they would be recognized. So Felix finally went to Yad Vashem. After watering a tree in the courtyard of the memorial building, in commemoration of those righteous people who had saved a Jewish life, they walked inside. Felix gave a speech in Hebrew and talked about people like the Puchalskis who had "saved Poland's soul."

"It is true," he said, "that the names on the plaques outside are mostly Polish. That was where most of Europe's Jews died, and that was where some Poles rose above the hatred and fear to risk everything – themselves and their families – to save the lives of innocent people." With that, the youngest Puchalski family member, Wanda, came to the front of the group. Without having prepared a speech, she spoke magnificently – from the heart – about Jews, about Israel, and why Israel must be strong. She mentioned how good she felt being there. She said that they were like one family; when she finished, everyone was in tears.

Then, at the chapel, where an eternal flame flickered, surrounded by names in the floor, names like Auschwitz, Buchenwald, and Treblinka, the son of Janova Puchalski's daughter Sabina approached the rabbi. After a few words, he returned to his family, and he and his aunts and uncles, the whole Puchalski family, all sank to their knees with their hands clasped and began praying in Polish: "Our Father who art in heaven, Hallowed be thy name…"

Here they were at Yad Vashem, on their knees in a Jewish sanctuary – the men in yarmulkes – praying a Catholic prayer in Polish! Their strength of character was obvious, just like Janova's.

The final chapter of our amazing hero's story was written in 1998 when he had the opportunity of closing a momentous circle in his life and in the story of the Jewish people. It came to his attention that a leading German electronics manufacturer was experiencing economic difficulties. The company was TEMIC Telefunken Microelectronic GmbH. At first, Felix was reluctant to get involved because of the company's history. Telefunken, which was once co-owned by AEG, had played an important role in the war effort. AEG, a crown jewel of the German electronics industry, had previously been owned by Jews! The company was formed in 1881 by Emil Rathenau to manufacture products based on Thomas Edison's patents. Rathenau's eldest son Walther was appointed Germany's only Jewish foreign minister in 1922, an amazing achievement in itself. But it was unfortunately short-lived, for later that year he was assassinated by the extreme right. The Nazis then nationalized AEG and developed it into its position of prominence in German manufacturing.

Vishay was now in a position to acquire the semiconductor business unit of TEMIC Telefunken Microelectronic for hundreds of millions of dollars. Felix, this once-hopeless Jewish boy, felt he had received a historic calling. After some difficult negotiations, involving attorneys on both sides, Vishay had the acquisition!

Felix felt again that he was closing a circle. Here he was, a Jewish refugee from Poland, ready to sign a multi-million-dollar deal to buy one of Germany's biggest companies – forty-six years after his ordeal of survival!

When the day finally came, Felix sat in the boardroom in Germany where the contract would be signed. He had signed many similar contracts in the past and made similar deals over the years, but this was different. This was a company created by a Jew and owned by the Jewish German foreign minister who had been murdered in cold blood. Then six million of Felix's fellow Jewish brethren had met the same fate. Now, another Jew – a Jew from Grodno, who had lost almost his entire family in Hitler's ovens – would regain control of the company.

Now in the boardroom, at the table where the executives and VIPs were seated, he hesitated before signing the contract. He hesitated for another moment. Then, slowly and deliberately, he put his hand in his pocket, pulled out a yarmulke, and placed it on his head.

Then he uttered these words in Hebrew in the presence of all the Germans there: "*Baruch atah A-do-nai E-lo-heinu melech ha'olam she'hecheyanu v'kiyemanu v'higiyanu la'zman hazeh*" (Blessed are You, Lord our God, King of the universe, Who has kept us in life, and has preserved us and enabled us to reach this season). He said it slowly and passionately, and then signed the contract. He was now the owner of the semiconductor business unit of TEMIC Telefunken Microelectronic. He had certainly come full circle, on many different levels. Today, if you visit Vishay's facility in northern Germany, you will see an Israeli flag there, proudly proclaiming its presence.

Dr. Felix Zandman, our hero, died in 2011, but his scientific and technological achievements are astounding. There are seventy patents to his name. His physics textbooks are used by many universities and have been translated into Chinese.

Our hero, a devoted Zionist, became an Israeli citizen in 1994. Felix was a member of Tel Aviv University's Board of Trustees and in 2004 its Zandman-Slaner School of Graduate Studies in Engineering was inaugurated.

A few years ago, Rabbi Yitzchak Kofman and his wife left Israel and moved to Grodno, Poland, to breathe new life into the few hundred Jews living there. Who was their greatest benefactor, helping rebuild the magnificent Jewish Community Center in Grodno? No one but our hero, the little boy once called Feivel, the little boy who was once hunted like an animal and who lost his entire family and community to monsters. He now helped create a Jewish renaissance in Grodno! Amazing!

The Jewish spirit and determination of Dr. Felix Zandman, his caring for his fellow man – taught him by his Grandma Tema – his zeal for life, his belief in God, will never – should never – be forgotten. He was truly a man for the ages!

6. *Simon Wiesenthal*
||||||||||||||||||||||||||||||||||||||||||||||||||||||

N o other hero of recent Jewish history has achieved greater renown than Simon Wiesenthal for his exploits in hunting down Nazi war criminals after World War II. Born in Buczacz, a small town in the Ukraine, in 1908, Simon eventually went to Prague and earned a degree in engineering in 1932 at age twenty-four. After marrying Cyla Mueller in 1936, he became an architect in Lvov, a profession he pursued for three years until the Russian army's occupation. The Russians murdered and imprisoned many members of his family in a Red purge of Jewish businesses. The Germans eventually replaced the Russian regime, and Simon and his wife, after evading execution by the Nazis, were arrested and interned in a railroad labor camp. The Nazis' Final Solution to the "Jewish Question" was soon in full operation, and in August 1942 Simon's mother was sent to the death camp at Belzec. By September, most of his and his wife's relatives– a total of eighty-nine members of both families – were dead, murdered by the Nazis.

Fortunately, Simon's wife fared well; she was able to pass as an Aryan because of her blond hair. So Simon arranged for her to be sent out of their prison camp in 1942, in a deal that he struck with the Polish underground. She survived the war doing forced labor and her true identity was never discovered.

Then Simon escaped the Ostbahn camp in 1943 at the age of thirty-four, before the German liquidation of its inmates. As fortunate as he was, however, he was later recaptured and sent to the Janowska concentration camp in June 1944. Luck again saved his life, as the German soldiers kept the few remaining inmates alive – otherwise, with no prisoners to guard, they would have been sent into combat, where

Germany was being overrun by the Red army. Out of the original 149,000 prisoners, only thirty-four survived the camp. They were then forced to march westward, to Mauthausen in upper Austria. Barely alive, weighing less than one hundred pounds, Simon feebly held on. The inmates, Simon among them, welcomed the American armored corps on May 5, 1945, as they liberated Mauthausen and its survivors.

After regaining his health, our hero was determined to bring the Nazis to justice. He gathered evidence on Nazi atrocities for the war crimes division of the US Army and also began working for the army's Office of Strategic Services and the Counter-Intelligence Corps. While all this was happening, he was unbelievably reunited in 1945 with his wife Cyla, whom he had thought dead (she had also thought he had died). Soon thereafter, a daughter, Pauline, was born; Simon's life was finally beginning anew after the horrors he and his wife had endured at the hands of the Nazis.

Soon, with the Cold War escalating, Russia and the United States lost interest in prosecuting German war criminals. Simon was left with very few files, and his volunteers drifted away in frustration, but one file remained that proved crucial to his efforts – that of Adolf Eichmann. This was the German officer who, as chief of the Nazis' Jewish Department, supervised the operations of the Final Solution. He was responsible for the deportation and murder of millions of European Jews and yet walked about a free man!

In his new offices at the Jewish Historical Documentation Center in Linz, Austria, our hero set out to pursue the elusive Eichmann. He continued his salaried relief and welfare work – and even ran an occupational training school for Hungarian refugees – to make a living and support his family, but his focus never wavered from Eichmann. A source in Argentina provided Simon with information that Eichmann was there. This valuable evidence was forwarded to Israel through the Israeli embassy in Vienna in 1954. But it was not until 1959, five years later, that Germany informed Israel of Eichmann's exact whereabouts: he was living under the assumed name of Ricardo Klement in Buenos Aires. From that point, Eichmann was quickly hunted down and captured by Israeli Mossad operatives. He was brought to Israel and found guilty of mass murder in a trial broadcast worldwide in 1961. He was executed on May 31, 1962.

Simon Wiesenthal was greatly encouraged by his success in helping to find Eichmann. He reopened the Jewish Documentation Center in Vienna and poured all his efforts into hunting war criminals. He had a small, sparsely furnished, barely heated office in downtown Vienna. It was very rudimentary, financed entirely by private funds. Simon's new focus, his next high-priority target, was Karl Silberbauer, the Gestapo officer who arrested Anne Frank – the fourteen-year-old Jewish girl who famously recorded the goings-on of her family and friends over the two years they spent in hiding in an attic, and who was then murdered by the Nazis. At the time, Dutch Nazi sympathizers were trying to discredit Frank's published diary as a fabrication. Simon was determined to prove them wrong. He finally located Silberbauer, then a police inspector in Vienna (of all places!), in 1963. "Yes," Silberbauer confessed. "I arrested Anne Frank."

Not long after, in 1966, sixteen SS officers were put on trial in Stuttgart for participating in the slaughter of Lvov's Jews – nine of them were found by Simon. Simon, a determined Nazi hunter, then located Franz Stangl, a noted Nazi murderer, after three years of undercover work. Stangl had been the commandant of Treblinka and Sobibor, two of the most infamous death camps in Poland. He was found in Brazil and imprisoned in West Germany in 1967. Stangl was then tried, convicted, and sentenced to life in prison; he died while incarcerated, justice again having been served.

It should be noted that Simon Wiesenthal was aided by a vast global network of friends, colleagues, and sympathizers, including, amazingly, German veterans repulsed by all they had witnessed during the war. Some information even came to him from former Nazis bringing to bear their grievances against other former Nazis – ex-Nazis turning against one another!

One former Nazi – a Jewish Nazi, no less! – came into Simon's service seeking personal redemption, and helped to capture the vicious

Nazi commandant Kurt Wiese. The story began in 1958 when a tall man with reddish-blond hair, who looked to be in his late thirties, paid a visit to Simon's office in Vienna. He was very nervous and uncomfortable and wore dark glasses to obscure his face. His name was Alex. He began telling his story to Simon, who flinched when this Aryan-looking stranger revealed to him that his father and grandfather had been Jewish. Not only that, but his grandfather had actually been a rabbi!

Alex had been very close to his father, but in 1938, when Germany invaded Austria, his father and his Catholic mother decided he must be protected; as a half-Jew he was in serious danger. He thus became the child of his uncle, an Aryan – not his father's son any longer.

If this wasn't hard enough for Simon to hear, Alex admitted that in 1940, at age eighteen, he joined the Waffen-SS, the elite police force of the Nazi Party! This he did at his uncle's suggestion in order to protect his Jewish father. Later, he found out that his actions hadn't made any difference. The Gestapo threatened his mother to divorce his father: "The mother of an SS man must not stay married to a Jew!" His father agreed, and after leaving her with all his assets, he was deported to a concentration camp.

Alex continued his story. He had not believed that Jews were being exterminated in great numbers until he was wounded and sent to recuperate in a Russian hospital. He shared a room with two other SS men who had been guards in a concentration camp. After Alex transferred to a smaller room with one of the guards, his roommate confided the whole truth – he was hospitalized because he had collapsed on the job; he could not go on after weeks of shooting women and children in cold blood.

A totally distraught Alex volunteered for patrol duty after his release from the hospital. He allowed himself to be captured by the Russians. He could no longer fight as a Waffen-SS elite soldier; he prayed for his Jewish father's safety.

After six years as a Russian POW, he returned to Austria. His mother had died and his father had disappeared – "along with millions of other Jews," he said sadly.

In Simon's office Alex was once again totally unnerved. He felt he didn't belong anywhere. He explained, "Am I an SS man? Am I a Jew? Am I a persecutor, or one of the persecuted?"

Simon tried to reassure him that his efforts to save his father were purely intentioned, but Alex replied, "To the Jews I am a damned SS man; for the others I'll always be a dirty Jew. I am the eternal bad guy."

Finally, he blurted out, "I came to see you because I feel I am a Jew. For myself and for you I am a Jew – but to the outside world I could remain an SS man and help you with your work! I feel I could be of some use."

After vetting the man's story, Simon began working with him. Alex joined the SS veterans' group, the Kameradschaft. To them, he would be the good German.

Then, in July 1969 an announcement on the radio shook Simon to the core: Colonel Kurt Wiese, under indictment for war crimes, had vanished in Cologne while out on bail. Simon was intimately familiar with this evil Nazi's background. Wiese had killed at least two hundred people in Grodno and Białystok, Poland, in 1942–1943, of whom eighty had been Jewish children. He had committed many other crimes as well, including killing the entire personnel of the Jewish hospital in Grodno, another forty souls. Even the Russians had cooperated in the prosecution of this evil Nazi killer, and now he was on the loose.

Simon went into action. He was determined to hunt Wiese down. Who was the first person he called? You guessed it – none other than Alex, who happened to be in Innsbruck, Austria, and heard that Wiese had escaped and traveled there as a "refugee." They were on his trail! Soon Alex found out from his fellow veterans that a comrade – Herbert von Trips, a former Gestapo *Kommissar* – had put Wiese up at his home in Graz, Austria. The next day, Alex reported that a Hubert Zimmerman, a man with a limp in his right leg, had gone from Graz to Semmering, a mountain resort south of Vienna. The following day, von Trips picked up Zimmerman at his hotel and drove to Vienna. Was Zimmerman actually Wiese? Alex and Simon were in constant contact during this crucial time. Thus, Alex was informed that Wiese was tall, fifty years old, wore a dark gray suit and glasses, and had a pronounced limp in his right leg. This matched his description of Zimmerman. They had their man.

Then, after three days of observing Wiese/Zimmerman, Alex reported that Wiese was in contact with the Egyptian embassy, probably to secure a visa to Egypt. From this report, Simon now knew Wiese's next move would be to Belgrade, Yugoslavia, by train, to get a visa from the Egyptian embassy there; he could fly straight on to Egypt from Belgrade. Time was now of the essence. What to do? They only had six hours to get Wiese arrested! The authorities in Vienna needed details from officials in Germany before acting on Wiese. Interpol in Austria was contacted, but time was running out. Simon made frantic calls to the Austrian minister of the interior and to other agencies, and then all that was left to do was wait and hope.

Finally, two hours later, at 3:18 p.m., the Austrian minister of the interior, Mr. Wiesinger, called again to officially verify the Wiese's identity. They were on Wiese's trail. They were going to send two officers speeding to Semmering by police car to catch Wiese's train! Simon was told the officers would board the train quietly, with no excitement at the station. Simon waited anxiously to see if his and Alex's efforts would pay off. Later, Alex came back to Vienna to tell him what he witnessed. "Wiese boarded the train from Vienna," he recounted.[13] "It was ready to leave three minutes later, when the two Austrian detectives arrived. The train was already moving, but they ran and managed to get aboard the last coach – the whistle blew, and the train disappeared into the tunnel."

So what happened on the train? Simon had heard that story directly from the detectives. Before the train stopped at the next station, the detectives walked through it and came to a compartment with a solitary man inside. His right leg appeared to be stretched out, they said. They watched him quietly. When the man got up to take a newspaper from the rack above, he limped with his right leg – yes! He was

---

13 This tale is recorded in Wiesenthal, *The Murderers Among Us.*

their man! They entered the compartment and stepped before him. "Herr Wiese," they said. Unaware, he nodded, then shook his head quickly – suddenly, they saw fear in his eyes. "My name is – " he blurted out. The detective responded, "We know who you are, Herr Wiese. You're under arrest."

Wiese told the police his story and gave the Austrian police the names of other comrades who helped him. All were arrested and indicted. This evil murderer and his *Kameraden* in Graz, Austria, were apprehended and our hero Simon Wiesenthal achieved justice again. Alex too, "Simon's eyes among the German veterans," was now fully a Jew again, truly, no longer "the eternal bad guy." He had redeemed his troubled past and his anguish over trying to protect his beloved father – whom he never saw again.

This is how Simon pieced together many of his cases. Simon perused every document and record he could get his hands on and heard the personal accounts of many survivors. He skillfully connected the most ambiguous, fragmented, and seemingly unrelated evidence to present thorough and solid cases to the authorities. If the authorities declined to act, either because of pro-Nazi sympathies or for other reasons, he would go to the press and media to publicize his findings. That publicity, along with outraged public opinion, usually got action – making it a powerful tool in his arsenal. Simon never gave up, and never gave quarter, in his quest for justice for the mass murderers of millions of Jews and other victims.

In essence, Simon Wiesenthal's indefatigable fight was against the world's indifference to the Nazis' crimes and its failure to call its perpetrators to account. From the day he was liberated from Mauthausen, he made it his life's work to hunt down Nazi war criminals and bring them to justice. His motto, his creed, was "Justice, not vengeance."

Our hero's many honors include decorations from the Austrian and French resistance movements, the Dutch Medal of Freedom, the Medal for Freedom of Luxemburg, the US Congressional Gold Medal, and the French Legion of Honor medal. Wiesenthal was also nominated for the Nobel Peace Prize in 1985 and knighted by Queen Elizabeth in 2004.

Once, when Simon was spending Shabbat at the home of a friend in New York, a wealthy jewelry manufacturer and former Mauthausen inmate, he was asked by his host, "Why didn't you resign and build houses? You'd be rich today. Why didn't you?" Simon then replied to his friend, "You're a religious man. You believe in God and life after death. I also believe. When we come to the other world and meet the millions of Jews who died in death camps and they ask us, 'What have you done?' there will be many, many answers. You will say, 'I became a jeweler,' another will say, 'I have smuggled coffee and American cigarettes,' another will say, 'I built houses' – but I, I will say, 'I didn't forget you!'"

Simon Wiesenthal did not forget. Today, his name and accomplishments are perpetuated by the Simon Wiesenthal Center in Los Angeles, California. The center was founded in 1977 through a gift from a Canadian businessman, Samuel Belzberg; Rabbi Marvin Hier has headed the organization since. The Wiesenthal Center has grown to 380,000 members, second in size only to B'nai B'rith International. In addition to combatting antisemitism worldwide, the center fervently promotes Zionist and Israeli interests. It also still advocates and demands the dauntless pursuit and punishment of Nazi war criminals even today, seventy years after the end of World War II.

In 1982, *Genocide*, a ninety-minute movie about the Holocaust that was co-produced by the center, was awarded the Academy Award for Best Documentary Feature. The center's Museum of Tolerance opened in 1993 to rave reviews and now attracts more than 350,000 visitors each year, including seventy thousand public and private school children. Simon Wiesenthal devoted his life to pursuing the perpetrators of the Holocaust. The center continues his work and goes to extraordinary lengths to prevent such a tragedy from happening again to any people, not only the Jewish people.

Our hero died on September 20, 2005, at his home in Vienna. He was ninety-six years old. His biographers credit him with locating

1,100 of Hitler's major and minor executioners and other Nazi war criminals since the end of World War II. Simon Wiesenthal dedicated his life to educating the world that the Nazis could not execute millions of people and go unpunished.

Part 4
||||||||||||||

AMAZING JEWISH HEROES
OF THE STATE OF ISRAEL

7. Theodor Herzl
||||||||||||||||||||||||||||||||||||||||

O ur next hero inspired the birth of Zionism and the Jewish state. In doing so, he gave new meaning to Jewish identity, both in Israel and throughout the world. Theodor Herzl, born May 2, 1860, in Budapest, Hungary, to a well-to-do family, undoubtedly became one of the world's greatest statesmen. He alone, it seems, grasped the nature of the threat posed by antisemitism some fifty years before the Holocaust. He would dedicate his entire life to saving the Jewish people from the clutches of antisemitic hatred.

After receiving a law degree from the University of Vienna, Theodor decided to pursue a career in writing. In 1891, he became the Paris correspondent for the *Neue Freie Presse*, a Viennese newspaper. There he came face-to-face with heightened daily antisemitic sentiment. He became increasingly uncomfortable with this issue, this cancer. Finally, while covering the 1894 trial of Alfred Dreyfus, an assimilated Jewish officer in the French army accused of treason, Theodor was appalled by the Parisian mobs shouting, "Death to the Jews!" in the streets. How, he wondered, could such hatred of Jews lie dormant in modern Parisians, especially when the Jews in France were fully emancipated members of society? Now he began to realize that this problem demanded establishing a nation-state for Jews and a political solution as well. But what to do?

He pondered the question and came to believe that only by establishing a state for the Jewish people could the distress and hatred of antisemitism be resolved. His pamphlet *Der Judenstaat* (The Jewish state), published in 1896, presented the case for his beliefs. However, not all Jews agreed with him – the Jewish masses in eastern Europe and Russia were enthusiastic, but many elite Jews in emancipated countries thought otherwise, believing that Zionism only affirmed Jewish separateness and would create more, not less, antisemitism. For them, assimilation was the preferred way to ensure an end to Jewish hatred.

Despite representing a minority of Jewish opinion, Theodor began to actively seek diplomatic ties to further his plans. Firstly, he attempted to secure a charter from the Turkish sultan for the rights of Jews to settle in Ottoman Palestine. Next, he sought international and local recognition of the rights of the Jewish people to live freely and have their own state in Palestine as well. This thought was the beginning of political Zionism, of which Theodor is considered the founder. He then proposed a program for collecting funds from Jews all over the world to support the establishment of a Jewish state.

Theodor viewed the future Jewish state as a model socialist state, one which would be based on the western European example, with an enlightened, neutral, peace-seeking society – a utopia built on cooperatives and the utilization of science and technology in its development. In addition, he saw the state as "a light unto the nations."

In 1897, he convened the first World Zionist Conference in Basel, Switzerland, and was elected its president. At the same conference in 1903, a schism arose amongst the delegates when discussion turned to a British suggestion that Uganda become a Jewish settlement (in lieu of Palestine). Many were opposed to this idea, which our hero Theodor personally endorsed as a temporary solution to evacuate Russian Jewry from rampant pogroms, and so the Uganda plan was set aside. But this incident hurt Theodor deeply because of the plan's complete rejection by his fellow members of the Zionist Congress.

In Vienna in 1904, Theodor developed pneumonia and heart problems. His extreme efforts on behalf of Zionism had taken their toll on his body, and he died of his maladies soon after, at the young age of forty-four. By then his catchphrase "If you will it, it is no fairy tale" had become the motto of the Zionist movement and his life's work had propelled the cause of Zionism toward realization.

Theodor Herzl's significance in Jewish history is as a leader and visionary in an era when antisemitism was a European cancer. He truly believed that once the Jewish state was a reality, once the Jewish people had a seat at the table, antisemitism would completely disappear. This assumption has certainly missed its mark. Today, years after the State of Israel's establishment in 1948 as a modern, democratic "light unto the nations," antisemitism and anti-Zionism are often interchangeable. In popular convention, there is no difference between the two – the Jews are Israel and Israel is the Jews. Theodor's keen analytical mind sought a rational solution for every problem; perhaps he oversimplified human nature in his quest for a solution to antisemitism. Clearly one cannot pinpoint a single root cause for such a complex phenomenon as antisemitism, which spans many cultures and thousands of years. However, Theodor's miscalculation in this regard does not detract from his incredible prediction of a Jewish calamity in Europe: he wrote in his diary that a tragedy would overtake even Hungarian Jews with brutality, and the longer it would take to come, the worse it would be. And he was absolutely right.

Today, we honor Theodor Herzl's achievements and vision, although this vision has not come to pass in its entirety. Now all Jews, wherever they live, are, in essence, represented by the Jewish state of Israel – which is as it should be. Indifference is no answer if you are a Jew living in this chaotic world, anywhere in a world where hatred still exists.

8. Ze'ev Jabotinsky
||||||||||||||||||||||||||||||||||||||||||||

P erhaps a lesser-known but no less significant Jewish hero is Vladimir (Ze'ev) Jabotinsky. His story certainly bears mentioning. Born in 1880 in Odessa, in Tsarist Russia, Ze'ev started at an early age to defend the Jews of Russia. He saw the impact of the infamous pogrom against the Jewish population in Kishinev in 1903, and afterward he became involved in organizing a defense militia.

Ze'ev was a writer, orator, and translator for Zionist issues. In 1925, he started the Revisionist Party in protest against the British Mandate's decision to exclude Transjordan from Palestine territory. He also founded Betar, the activist Zionist youth movement joined by future prime minister Menachem Begin at a young age; its purpose was to teach Hebrew language and culture and to confront and deal with antisemitism using different methods of self-defense. Ze'ev was a delegate at the Sixth Zionist Congress, where he was enthralled with Theodor Herzl and the fervor of the Zionist activists – even though Herzl's "Uganda Plan" (to establish a Jewish homeland in Africa) was voted down at the time. Ze'ev became the foremost proponent of and journalist for Hebrew culture, language, and Zionism in the Russian Jewish communities. Here is his story.

Ze'ev was born into a Yiddish-speaking middle-class household. His father was a grain agent, expediting the shipment of wheat from Russia to western Europe. Sadly, Ze'ev was only six years old when his father died of cancer after lingering for many months in a German hospital.

The family's savings were considerably diminished, the home very modest, but even so Ze'ev was high-spirited, self-confident, and inquisitive. As a young boy, he roamed the streets of Odessa without supervision and often played hooky from school. Once, when asked who his father was, so he could be brought home and punished for some misbehavior, he replied, "I'm just me.[I have no father.]"[14] To earn extra money, he wrote compositions for classmates.

He came from a religious home, where his mother kept kosher and lit the Shabbat candles every Friday evening. He also learned to speak Hebrew very well from his mother. He celebrated his bar mitzvah at thirteen, but surprisingly had no continuing contact with Judaism after that. Odessa was an international city with minimal antisemitism. Thus, Ze'ev grew up against a backdrop of assimilation – not one of the shtetl, or strong Jewish influences.

Ze'ev developed a liking for journalism at an early age; this motivated him, at eighteen, to leave Odessa to study law in Rome (he spoke eight languages fluently). While in school there, he also took a job as a foreign correspondent to several Russian newspapers, using the literary pseudonym "Altalena,"[15] and his brilliance as a writer was soon recognized. In addition, he began writing plays and articles about the Jewish condition. But the massive 1903 pogrom in Kishinev– a heavily populated Jewish town one hundred miles northwest of Odessa – commanded Ze'ev's attention as a journalist and as a Jew. He was angry and determined not to be passive, so he wrote a letter to the organized Jewish community demanding action – the formation of a Jewish self-defense force. Little did he know that such an organization already existed. They expressed interest in him and he quickly responded. From that point forward he became involved in their activities, composing proclamations, raising money, purchasing weapons, even teaching

---

14 This quotation and all that follow in this chapter are noted in Hillel Halkin, *Jabotinsky: A Life* (New Haven, CT: Yale University Press, 2014).

15 *Altalena* was later appropriated as the name of the ship chartered by the Irgun (Irgun Zva'i Leumi, the National Military Organization paramilitary in Palestine that Menachem Begin commanded) to convey Jewish Holocaust survivors and weaponry to Israel in June 1948. When the *Altalena* reached the coast of Israel, it was fired upon by the newly formed, Haganah-led IDF, and sixteen Irgun fighters were killed. The name *Altalena* means "seesaw" in Italian.

volunteers to be patrol officers who could shoot guns effectively. This would be his initiation into the fight for Jewish self-defense and independence.

But why did he begin this fight? Because our hero, who had begun speaking out to his community and to others throughout Russia, now believed, and said clearly,

> We are a people [and] you may as well be angry with your parents for having brought you into the world as wish to be excused from belonging to your people.... Life is always a war. The weak are treated with contempt. The bug squashed beneath someone's foot does not feel insulted; but men are sovereign even if exaggerated egotism can drive them to suicidal extremes.

He encouraged Jewish activism in Russia, in Palestine, and elsewhere in the Diaspora: "Jews must take their destiny into their own hands." Ze'ev had found his calling – he was going to make a difference!

Ze'ev's emergence as a Zionist voice brought him to the Sixth Zionist Congress in Basel, Switzerland, in August 1903, as a delegate and press correspondent. He was only twenty-three years old – still a very young man! At this Congress, Ze'ev first heard Theodor Herzl speak. Enchanted, he called Herzl "the most interesting-looking man I've ever seen," with a manner "sublimely courageous." He went on to say that Herzl was "unbending and magnificent. He has a profile like an Assyrian king's in an old bas-relief.... His oratory is not particularly emphatic – yet he outperforms all others... a man of mediocre abilities who is nonetheless a great figure – a genius of no special talents." Ze'ev now had a hero to put on a pedestal – from this point on, Zionism would be the focus of his life's work. From 1902, he had toured the length and breadth of Russia, spreading the Hebrew language and culture; he was quickly becoming the country's foremost Zionist lecturer (especially following Herzl's death in 1904).

While engaged in these diverse activities – writing, lecturing, organizing, going town to town – he found time to woo, and finally marry, his childhood friend Ania Gelperin. He knew this "great, rock-ribbed soul...could always be counted on in a pinch."

In 1908, Ze'ev was traveling through Turkey as a correspondent when he decided to detour to Palestine to see the Jewish agricultural settlements around the Galilee. Here, he viewed the terrain and realized that Palestine would not be given to the Jews by anyone, but that they would have to take it for themselves. The hostility toward the Jews in Europe, in Russia, and in Serbia, convinced him that it was "every people for itself."

By 1910, Ze'ev was devoting less time to literature and writing and more to the pursuit of Zionism. Another writer of that time, Simon Yoshkevitch, would lament the whisking away of "another Odessan, a God-given talent who could have been an eagle of Russian literature." But for our hero, this was his choice. "Politics are my greatest gift and talent," he said to Chaim Weizmann's wife Vera at a Zionist conference in 1910.

In 1914, after the outbreak of World War I, Ze'ev worked in Egypt as a war correspondent. There he saw many thousands of Jewish refugees from Palestine. (The Turkish authorities in Palestine had issued an ultimatum to its Jews – accept Ottoman citizenship or be deported. These good Jews in Egypt formed a microcosm of Palestine's Jewry: Ashkenazi and Sephardic, religious and non-religious.) In Egypt he also met a certain Joseph Trumpeldor. Trumpeldor, deeply Russian and a staunch Jewish patriot, was a high-ranking military officer (in fact, the highest ranking Jew in the Russian military) who had immigrated to Palestine in 1912. Ze'ev had already known fame as a correspondent in Rome, a composer, a writer of plays, and a war correspondent. Now he decided to embark on a new challenge: creating a Jewish Legion with his new friend and fellow pioneer Trumpeldor.

Ze'ev wanted a full Jewish Legion that would be incorporated into the British army to help fight the Turkish in Palestine but beholden to no one; he traveled to London, where in August 1917 the British agreed to his request. This came about despite much opposition from the Zionist Party (in the person of David Ben-Gurion), the English

Zionist Party (which wanted no Jewish military), the British government, and the eastern European Jewish immigrants (who feared conscription into the Legion ahead of British nationals).

Ze'ev was thirty-seven in July 1917 when he was finally given the go-ahead to fight the Turks in Palestine. The volunteer Jewish Legion would join the Royal Fusiliers as the 38th Battalion. It had eight hundred soldiers, kosher food, and a rabbi. Ze'ev soon became a second lieutenant and sailed to Alexandria, Egypt, for the mission to take Palestine from the Turks. Eventually, three Jewish battalions participated in the complete destruction of the Turkish army and the retaking of the Holy Land. At the same time, the Balfour Declaration had been issued (regarding the Brits' positive esteem for the creation of a Jewish national homeland), which should have been a great source of joy for our Ze'ev, but he instead felt profoundly disappointed because the Jewish Legion hadn't really played a significant role in the Turks' military defeat.

Ze'ev harbored a deep-seated sense of failure and fought major depression over his belief that he had not been a dedicated, attentive husband. He had given up his writings, his plays, his organizing of Zionism, and his political life, all to be a military man, an officer – and now he felt empty, with nothing to do and nothing but time on his hands in Palestine.

Ze'ev finally reunited with his wife Ania and son Eri in Palestine, after the war, and eventually settled in Jerusalem. The Jewish Legion and its soldiers had become demoralized, not really functioning as a meaningful military in Palestine, which was now under the control of the British. Even Ze'ev, now a civilian, was leery of British intentions in Palestine in 1920. And at this point, skirmishes began to occur with Arabs, who were fearful of Jewish immigration "stoking the fire." So when the British accused former Jewish Legionnaires, now the Haganah,[16] of the illegal possession of weapons, Jabotinsky (a former lawyer) was also arrested.

---

16 Haganah means "defense." The Haganah served as the self-defense force for Jewish settlements in Palestine and took on the characteristics of a military force during the later years of the British Mandate. The Haganah was led by and aligned with David Ben-Gurion and the Labor Party.

Following his trial, Ze'ev was sentenced to *fifteen years* in prison! He served three months in Acre Prison, and then a new civilian British administration pardoned all of Acre's prisoners. After his release Ze'ev became a national hero, lionized by the Jewish press all over the world. Unfortunately, his good friend Joseph Trumpeldor had been killed defending a settlement in Upper Galilee that had been overrun by Bedouin Arabs. Ze'ev had admired Trumpeldor as a great soldier who fought valiantly for the cause – the Zionist dream.

Later, in 1923, Ze'ev broke with the Zionist Left, who opposed the use of the "sword and the gun," and he formed the Betar youth movement in Riga, Latvia. Betar was an acronym for Brit Trumpeldor (the Trumpeldor league).[17]

It should be noted here that Ze'ev Jabotinsky was a man of exceptional and versatile talents, an original thinker, and a powerful political leader. His foray into militarism was based on a sincere, genuine belief that the use of force to curb Palestinian Arab nationalism needed to be part of Zionist thinking. This was at odds with some Jewish leaders, including Chaim Weizmann and David Ben-Gurion (see chapter 9), then influential in the World Zionist Organization, who felt that British support alone was necessary to achieve their goals. In 1925, Ze'ev founded the Revisionist Zionist party, a political organ he hoped would operate according to these beliefs.

As the leader of Betar, Ze'ev's aims were to educate its young members and instill in them a military and nationalistic spirit. So our hero, who was never afraid to speak his mind publicly, strategically shaped the Zionist movement's attitude toward the Palestinian Arabs. Unlike Ben-Gurion and Moshe Sharett, who thought the Arabs could be bribed into releasing their country and granting their rights – with British help – Jabotinsky firmly believed that the clash between Jewish and Arab Palestinian nationalism was inevitable and should not be ignored. In 1923, Ze'ev had stated, "The Arabs loved their country as

---

17 Betar is also the name of the village where Jewish fighters of the Bar Kochba Revolt had stood against the Romans thousands of years before; see chapter 1.

much as the Jews. Instinctively, they understand Zionist aspirations very well, and their decision to resist them was only natural.... No agreement was possible with the Palestinian Arabs; they would accept Zionism only when they found themselves up against an 'iron wall,' when they realize they had no alternative but to accept Jewish settlement."[18] This attitude has dictated Israel's policies toward the Palestinian Arabs from the 1930s to the present day.

So our hero Ze'ev nurtured and developed Betar from a fledgling movement to one that would represent the face of a Hebrew generation yearning for a national rejuvenation – a Jewish state.

Theodor Herzl had had the dream; men like Ze'ev were destined to see it through. So in 1928, he coined the Hebrew word *hadar* (Jewish dignity). Dignity, pride of bearing, majesty – these attributes, properly applied to daily life, would over time heal the beleaguered Jews of their Diaspora experiences and cultivate a nation of "new Jews." These same qualities were fine-tuned by our Menachem Begin (see chapter 11), who idolized Ze'ev and was inspired by his speeches and writings.

In 1935, Ze'ev's Revisionist Party feuded with Ben-Gurion's Labor Zionists in eastern Europe. The Nazi threat in Germany was growing. It was Ze'ev's talents as a captivating speaker and a great delegator of responsibility with intellectual curiosity and an artist's imagination – versus Ben-Gurion, the more abrasive personality, the more disciplined, a lover of facts and detail, intensely curious. They respected each other, while remaining scornful of each other, as they nevertheless shared a common goal – a Jewish state. Ultimately, Ben-Gurion's liberal left Mapai Party took control of the Zionist organization.

Ze'ev's loss in this fight, though difficult, left him time to pursue his passion of writing literature. But in 1935 the Mapai-led World Zionist Organization, the WZO, voted to outlaw any extra-organizational operations in an attempt to restrict illegal Jewish immigration to Palestine, which Ze'ev and like-minded Zionist thinkers eagerly

---

18 Vladimir Jabotinsky, "The Iron Wall," *Jewish Virtual Library*, first published November 4, 1923, accessed March 21, 2016, http://www. jewishvirtuallibrary.org/jsource/Zionism/ironwall.html.

promoted (even though just one year prior, in 1934, Ze'ev and Ben-Gurion had agreed to respect each other's views on immigration, and their respective parties' views). For many, this was the final straw. They boycotted the Mapai-led Zionist organization, and Ze'ev was free to form the New Zionists Organization, the NZO, in April 1935. Its goal was to conduct its own political activity for free immigration and the establishment of a Jewish state.

In 1935, Jabotinsky gave the keynote address at the NZO's first congress, calling for the conclusion of the Diaspora by means of a large-scale "evacuation" of world Jewry to a future Jewish state. Remember again that this was 1935; Europe was seething with antisemitism, and the Nazis were growing in power in Germany. Ze'ev viewed Zionism not merely as an antidote to Jewish exile, but a final end to it. But in Poland, and other countries, he was – unbelievably – accused of aiding and abetting antisemites in his fervor for Jewish mass immigration. Even Theodor Herzl had assumed the same – that the Diaspora would wither with the establishment of a Jewish state. Jabotinsky also reached out to Orthodox Jews as well, speaking of "a second Exodus from Egypt" and the "birth pangs of national redemption." Now, at age fifty-five, Ze'ev moved the NZO to London, along with his family. (Ze'ev could not make his home in Palestine because in 1929 the British had banned him from ever again stepping foot in the territory.)

As a side note, Ze'ev had written a remarkable novel in 1926 (in Russian), called *Samson the Nazarite*. Its theme was an imaginative tour of ancient Palestine, from which the State of Israel emerged, and Ze'ev's conflicts with these events. Now in London, but no longer writing for newspapers (and therefore with no income), he helped the Revisionist Party out of his personal funds. But as luck would have it, a check arrived one day from Paramount Pictures for $666 (a nice amount in those days) for the film rights to *Samson*. It was made into a movie (listing Ze'ev in the credits!) starring Victor Mature and Hedy Lamarr.[19] The movie grossed $11 million on its release in 1949.

---

19 Our hero Ze'ev, when he wrote the book *Samson the Nazarite,* had no idea it would be made into a movie, still less who its star would be. The female

In November 1938, Germany was deporting twenty thousand Jews to concentration camps, and Jews in Soviet Russia were subjected to brutal repression. In Poland, Lithuania, Latvia, Romania, and Hungary, Jews faced discrimination, daily attacks, and starvation. A new war in Europe was on the horizon. What would happen to the Jewish population?

Ben-Gurion, after a visit to London, was finally on board with Ze'ev: socialism could wait; a Jewish state, which would save as many Jews as possible, was the immediate priority – won by force of arms if necessary – regardless of the odds against it. Our hero needed to act, and quickly. Immigrants from Germany, Russia, Romania, and Lithuania had little interest in his policies; antisemitism in some cases was still just under the surface in those regions. Finally, in Poland, an agreement was reached, allowing Betar and Irgun training camps to function, obtain arms, and help Polish Jews leave for Palestine. Still, Ze'ev was upset with European Jewry for not uprooting themselves and embracing Zionism more aggressively. He even suggested an armed revolt against the British, using the Haganah, and then bringing thousands of immigrants to Palestine – but it was not going to happen for him, unfortunately.

Germany invaded Poland in 1939, and then all bets were off. Still, Ze'ev envisioned a Jewish army of 100,000 men fighting against the Axis

---

lead, Hedy Lamarr, an Austrian Jew, was born Hedy Kiesler in Vienna to a well-to-do banker father who doted on her. She began acting at a young age, finally landing a minor film role at age fifteen. Hedy wanted to be famous, so she eventually sought out Louis Mayer of MGM on a cruise ship to the United States and convinced him to hire her. She became a star after changing her last name, but her great interest was inventing, of all things! When German subs were sinking passenger ships as well as transport vessels, she zeroed in on torpedoes. She wanted to make sure Allied torpedoes found their mark without going astray; to achieve this goal, she invented a "spread spectrum radio" with a co-inventor, composer George Antheil. It was submitted to the US Navy and filed away for years. Finally, after World War II, her invention, now known as a "sonobuoy," would be used with sonar to detect submarines. She was finally honored for this achievement in her early eighties – to which she said, "It's about time." The life story of this beautiful actress is recounted in *Hedy's Folly*, a book by Richard Rhodes (New York: Vintage Books, 2011).

powers. This would arouse worldwide sympathy for a Zionist state, he believed, but unfortunately it did not come about. The NZO had diminished in power, and his command influence had melted away.

Disappointed and unhappy, Ze'ev moved to New York City in March 1940 with his family. His goal was to raise funds and promote a Jewish army. He soon found out, however, that American Jews were in an isolationist mood and proud of it – they certainly were not going to send their sons to fight a foreign war! In New York, his disappointment with American Jews caused him much distress and heartbreak. In addition, he had little money and his health was deteriorating; he had developed heart problems and diabetes. In July 1940, his doctors had advised him to rest, to get away, and he did, traveling to the Catskills to visit a Betar summer camp. Ze'ev, who had never been truly religious, asked to be taught Kol Nidre, the solemn prayer sung on Yom Kippur, the holiest day of the year. He was fluent in Hebrew, so he learned the prayer easily while on his journey to the camp. He was returning to his roots – was this a premonition?

He arrived at the Betar camp, and after reviewing an honor guard he collapsed and died. He was not quite sixty. One of his last requests was that if he was buried outside Eretz Israel, he would someday be returned there at the order of a Jewish government in that country – a country and government that he knew in his heart and soul would surely come to be.

That wish came true when, many years later, Menachem Begin, his protégé and at the time head of the opposition in the Israeli parliament, pressed Prime Minister Levi Eshkol to reinter the Betar leader. Ze'ev and his wife Ania received full military honors when they were returned to Israel and were buried at Mt. Herzl cemetery in 1964. (She was buried beside him when she died in 1949; she did not want to leave him alone.)

Ze'ev Jabotinsky was a truly amazing man, a man of many talents, a powerful political leader and speaker, and a great literary light. He always spoke his mind and certainly influenced the strategic conduct of the Zionist movement with respect to the Arab Palestinian people.

He was totally at odds with leaders like David Ben-Gurion and Moshe Sharett, who felt that the Arabs could be persuaded into giving up their country and their rights – Ze'ev felt deeply that Jewish justice should prevail over Arab rights. He advocated the use of force to curb the inevitable clash between Jewish and Arab Palestinian nationalism. In 1923, he stated, "The Palestinian Arabs would accept Zionism only when they found themselves up against an 'iron wall,' when they realize they had no alternative but to accept Jewish settlement [a Jewish state]."

Although Ze'ev Jabotinsky was never a leader of a Jewish state, he foresaw much of what eventually came to pass in it. He was a dreamer, yes, and a militaristic man, a believer in individualism, and a fiery nationalist – all these things – but most of all, our hero was a believer in the dream of a Jewish state. He dedicated his life and all his energies to that goal.

Rest in peace, our hero Ze'ev Jabotinsky.

9. David Ben-Gurion
||||||||||||||||||||||||||||||||||||||||||||||||||

The story of David Ben-Gurion is more than just the story of an extraordinary man; it is a unique story of biblical prophecy, of the eternal dream of the Jewish people's desire to be at last in their homeland after a centuries-long diaspora. David's deep belief in and passion for Zionism, his fears, and his frustrations are all part of the fabric and the essence of this great man.

Ben-Gurion was a modern Jewish biblical figure, like a Moses or Isaiah, who was compelled and destined to be part of and create a new Jewish state to be a "light unto the nations." His mission was always before him and nothing could distract him, including his most beloved, the love of his life, Rachel Nelkin. He persevered despite many obstacles – primary of which were the heavy burdens of the Holocaust and World War II. But he triumphed and established the State of Israel in May 1948, built a great army, and brought his people home at last. Here is his story.

From the time David Green, at the age of three, climbed onto his brilliant grandfather's knee and began learning Hebrew, his view of the world was formed. The Yiddish spoken in his home evolved into Hebrew, the language of the Bible, and David learned quickly. How quickly? When David showed up for *cheder* (Jewish religious elementary school) at age four, his teacher was amazed at his brilliance. When David, soon after, repeated a page from the Bible from memory after hearing a classmate recite it, the teacher knew David was by far the most gifted child in the class!

David's father Avigdor was an unlicensed attorney who represented clients entangled in government problems. He was an elegant man who believed that self-discipline and a good appearance were the keys to respectability. Like his own father, Zvi Green, along with most Jews in his village in Poland, Avigdor dreamed of aliyah ("going up" to Eretz Israel), a return to Zion – a homeland for Jews – and saw it as the only solution to Jewish oppression and insecurity in the Diaspora.

David Green was born in 1886 in a *shtetl* called Plonsk in Russian Poland. Over the years Russian antisemitism had reared its ugly head many times, but Plonsk had been spared thus far. The Jews of Plonsk, however, were still aware that the pogroms might begin anew at any time under Tsar Alexander III. In this dangerous environment, David excelled in elementary school and was soon chosen to attend a school for gifted children, where he studied the Bible, the Talmud, and Hebrew grammar full-time. While immersed in these studies, David always yearned for the Jewish people's return to Eretz Israel – for he was a committed Zionist at the age of eight!

David's early educational requirements included attending a *beit midrash* (a "house of learning," a Jewish study hall), where, on the Sabbath, all the town's elite intellectuals and businessmen would sit and pray for deliverance to Zion. This study hall gave David insight into how the town's elite could be motivated to evolve into ardent Zionists. David's education continually evolved as well, and even socialist books and Russian books on culture fascinated him deeply at his young age. He loved to learn and to study.

When David was ten, an event took place that would forever shape him and his dreams of a Jewish homeland. A rumor had begun in his town that the Redeemer had come! He was, supposedly, tall and handsome, with a black beard. His name? Dr. Herzl.

Theodor Herzl's visionary plan of a real Jewish home, with financing from Jewish international banks, completely swept through the Jewish world – all the way to Plonsk.

Our hero David, as a young boy, was ecstatic at this news. It motivated him, at age eleven, to start a youngsters' Zionist society. But tragedy soon struck his family – his mother Sheindel died in childbirth. David, deeply hurt, became more self-reliant and assertive. He knew at age twelve that he needed someone to fill this emotional void, and he

soon met Rachel Nelkin – the prettiest girl in Plonsk, and the daughter of a Hassidic rabbi, of all things! And although most Hassidim
did not endorse Zionism, believing that the Jewish people should not
take political action to establish a homeland without the advent of the
Redeemer, Rachel's father did. David and Rachel became good friends
despite the criticism of Plonsk's Jewish elders, who had warned the
(non-Zionist) Hassidim not to mix with Zionists like David and his
family, who associated with the local non-Jews. David certainly objected to their condemnation of Zionism and vowed to start a school
for teaching Hebrew to poor children. He wanted Hebrew to be the
Jews' everyday tongue, a precursor to his dream of a Jewish state whose
citizens would all speak Hebrew!

David enlisted his good friends Shmuel and Shlomo for this, and
despite their families' objections, the three began their quest. One day
in December 1900, David announced at the *beit midrash* sanctuary,
before a group of thirty comrades, the birth of the "Ezra Society" –
named after Ezra the Prophet, who founded the Second Temple. At
fourteen years of age, our hero was already an emerging leader.

The founders of the Ezra Society began knocking on the doors of
the poorest Jewish homes, offering to teach the children Hebrew. There
were some objections, but soon 150 children began attending classes
for one and a half hours a day. David would read Zionist poems he
had written himself, in Hebrew, and conduct Bible study and lessons.
Soon, many young people in Plonsk could be heard speaking Hebrew
with family and friends; they had learned it phonetically; it was like a
symphonic sound.

David and his friends achieved a degree of success, but the Yiddish-
speaking Hassidim were outraged. They denounced Zionism and its
revival of Hebrew as a spoken language as heresy. But David Green
now believed more than ever that creating a morally and intellectually
superior nation-state could give Zionism a new, visionary dimension.
He believed that ultimate power came from the backing of the impoverished masses. David had been influenced by his family, his books
on socialism, his shtetl, and his religion. He now linked Zionism and

socialism as his model, his goal. David Green had already set forth to pursue his life's calling. How many of us could be so forward-thinking, so clear in our goals, at such an early age?

David was now smitten with Rachel Nelkin, more so than even he could understand. "I was still a boy, about twelve years old, and was already in love..." he wrote in his late teens. "My love was young like an early spring bird, but it grew in the course of time and burned like a flame – and last summer I found out that she loves me."[20] David even wrote love poems about Rachel, but he knew that her family disapproved of him even then. Astonishingly, David and his Zionist friends, Shmuel Fuchs and Shlomo Zemach, therefore decided that now was the time for them to go to Palestine! Here they were, barely past their bar mitzvahs, and their minds were made up! But in the end only Shmuel Fuchs left Plonsk for Palestine – the only one to defy his family. David decided to go his own way to Warsaw, not so far away that he could not return to Plonsk in a few hours to see his beloved Rachel.

In Warsaw, lonely and without money, David found a teaching job, but was ultimately denied the post because of Russian "Jewish quotas." He then found another job teaching Hebrew, to keep him in Warsaw. He tried and failed to inaugurate another Ezra society; he was not happy in his new environs. All his dreams, it seemed, were on hold. He was despondent and depressed.

Finally, his old friend Shlomo Zemach visited him, and announced his plans to go to Palestine. Now, even though Shlomo's father was very adamant against this, even visiting David in Warsaw to try to stop the planned trip, David bade Shlomo a private farewell and told him he would certainly go to Eretz Israel and the three of them would meet there one day soon. A few weeks later, David opened a letter from Shlomo telling of his arrival in Palestine and his journey to a Jewish settlement called Rishon LeZion. He told David he was working and

---

20 This quotation and all that follow in this chapter are noted in Dan Kurzman, *Ben-Gurion: Prophet of Fire* (New York: Simon and Schuster, 1983) unless otherwise indicated.

described the beauty of the land – the mountains, the sunlit sea, the dazzling flowers, the golden fruit. David was overwhelmed with joy at the news.

David was still in Warsaw, where Polish socialists were actively demonstrating against the government. These revolutionaries, by smashing stores and carrying rifles and stones, had motivated their Cossack masters to rein them in and crush them. But this revolutionary movement also captured David's attention, for his goal was to build an exemplary Jewish state, which would be a "light unto the nations" and lead to the redemption of all – including the Poles. But at the same time, he saw many, many Jews who were anti-Zionists, and it saddened him very deeply.

David's remaining time in Warsaw was spent working with the Workers of Zion (Po'alei Zion) organization, whose aim was to build a socialist state in Palestine. He worked diligently to organize Jewish workers and instill Zionism in them. These activities allowed David to gain experience as a labor leader and sharpened his image for a future central role in Zionist affairs. After organizing a strike of seamstresses in Plonsk, his hometown, and seeing the judge side with the workers, David recognized the power of labor. He perceived the potential of a mighty labor movement in Palestine, one that would help build his dream state.

Now this young activist also realized that labor unions alone could not protect Jews, and soon formed a Jewish defense organization to arm and defend Jews against the Russian police. By challenging the police and intimidating them, he had triumphed. He had now become even more of a leader in the Jewish community, more respected, someone to be reckoned with.

Finally – finally! – David's dream of going to Palestine was realized. He left Poland and arrived in Palestine on September 7, 1906. He was nearly twenty years old. With him was Rachel Nelkin, the love of his life. They had left from Plonsk and taken a ship – an old tub – from Odessa. While en route, they endured antisemitic treatment from the crew. They were treated poorly, but they persevered and soon arrived in Eretz Israel. David was amazed at the number of Arabs working at menial jobs, but when he saw signs in Hebrew on the shops, stores, and restaurants, he felt waves of joy. This is what he had come for. This would be his homeland!

He finally settled in Petah Tikvah, a desolate settlement surrounded by orange and olive groves that housed 250 families. David and his friend Shlomo found the work very difficult, and David soon contracted malaria. Even though he was sick, he would not allow the illness to deter him. He endured hard work, malaria, and hunger, all the while knowing this was why he came to Eretz Israel. Rachel was also having a hard time, but David had decided to stop seeing her, despite his loneliness. David was still torn between his love for Rachel and his dream, but his commitment to Zionism would always trump his personal life and happiness. Rachel knew she had to make her own life without her beloved David!

David soon decided to channel his energies into village politics. He became a leader of the local Po'alei Zion – a socialist movement of Zionist workers in various countries across Europe . He ultimately desired to use his growing political stature to merge two political parties that formed from Po'alei Zion (Mapai and the Socialist party) into a single movement. This would be the foundation of the political structure that would one day be Israel.

Over the next year or so, David met with opposition to his dreams for Jewish nationalism. He fought for workers' rights and backed down before no one, sometimes alienating his own comrades. He was tough – and determined.

David wound up in Sejera, a settlement in Galilee where Shlomo had previously worked. This was a kibbutz (a cooperative farm) where Jews from all over the world embraced Judaism and worked the land. David thrived in this new environment, where everyone worked together, men and women, pulling together! He would write about this time that in Sejera, "I found the environment that I had sought so long – no shopkeepers or speculators, no more Jewish hirelings or idlers living on the labor of others."

David thrived at Sejera, but he also was sad – his relationship with Rachel had ended, he was away from his family, and, worst of all, he was shunned by his comrades and not accepted as a leader on the farm. Despondent, he went home to Poland and the love of family. There, suddenly, he was conscripted for military duty in the Russian army, and ordered to report for training. Serving in the military, where antisemitism was rampant and brutal, meant twenty years of hard service. So he had no choice but to desert, but before leaving Poland, David urged his father and his family members to follow him to Palestine – back to Sejera. Again, he urged and implored them to come.

David arrived in December 1909 at Jaffa, and journeyed to the Galilee and a colony called Kinneret. There he toiled hard, and soon, the following year, he drifted back to Sejera again. Here he encountered a situation where foreigners, Ottoman Circassians who guarded the perimeters of the cooperative, were deeply resented by the Jewish workers. To avoid trouble, our hero arranged for the Jewish workers to secure guns to protect themselves against this potential danger. David's leadership skills were now on full display, and he became the commander of security at Sejera.

This event, and another incident later that year, made David realize that Jews needed to be vigilant against the Arabs – who, it seems, were regularly marauding and attacking Jewish settlements. David had to constantly fight the kibbutz officials, who wanted to negotiate with and placate the Arabs, to talk things over, but not with guns. David was firm that "the Jews would never stand on their own as long as they had to depend on appeasement and other people's guns."

Our hero's mantra and calling had been clearly defined, but fate intervened again to help him on his way. In 1910, at a Zionist conference in Jaffa, David's old friend from Poland, Yitzchak Ben-Zvi, offered him the chance to join the editorial board of *Hayahadut* (Unity), a Hebrew-language socialist newspaper. At the same time, he learned that his beloved Rachel had married another man and had had a child with him. He was torn, but he knew he had to move forward – he must take the job! So our hero, twenty-four years old, left for Jerusalem; his years of farm work were over, his life of hard labor now behind him.

There were seventy-five thousand inhabitants of Jerusalem in 1912, of which forty-eight thousand were Jewish, seventeen thousand Christian, and ten thousand Muslim. The newspaper he now worked for reflected his views and was the voice of the vigorous socialist Labor Party. David was now able to express his political views in a newspaper, but he was frustrated that his political and organizational skills were not being honed or utilized. He still strived to realize his dream, the creation of a Jewish state in Palestine, but lamented losing the love of his life, Rachel, to his single-mindedness. However, realizing this only stiffened his resolve. He needed to continue to move forward toward his goal – he would not be deterred!

While writing for the paper, David decided on a pen name that would also become his legal name – David Ben-Gurion (naming himself after Yosef Ben-Gurion, a leader of the Jewish revolt against the Romans in 66 CE; its literal meaning is "lion cub"). He liked it; it seemed to fit his growling, aggressive personality.

David saw that Turkey and the Ottoman Empire were changing – a new democracy was emerging. He believed that this new entity might be the catalyst for carving out an opening for Jews to create their own autonomous state as well. David felt he could influence this change by studying law in Turkey, and he began to do so in 1912 with his friend Yitzchak Ben-Zvi. They enrolled at the University of Constantinople after learning the Turkish language, which David did very quickly. David's aim was to have a political career in Turkey when he graduated. He sincerely believed that the emerging democratic Turkey could help produce a Jewish state.

In July 1914, David sailed back to Palestine on a Russian ship on a short vacation from school. On board, he heard that war had broken out! Russia was now at war with Germany, and their ship could be seized by German warships at any moment! But as luck would have it, David made it safely to Palestine, after a detour to Alexandria, Egypt.

What would he do next? If the Turks joined Germany in the war, what would the Jews do? Turkey had always been tolerant of Jews, so David resolutely believed the Jews must stand with Turkey! Why? Because Russia had been the worst oppressor of Jews. But David's fate, along with that of his fellow Jews, was sealed when Jamal Pasha, Turkey's toughest military leader, sailed into Jaffa and took command of Palestine. David soon realized that Turkey considered all Jews enemies – Zionists could even be executed!

David, as a Zionist leader, was sure to be arrested, and he was, in 1915. After being released from prison, David was forced into exile, courtesy of Jamal Pasha. Before leaving for exile David met an Arab student also being detained by the Turks. David was asked by the student why he had been arrested. He replied that it had been on orders from Jamal Pasha. The Arab then replied to him that as a friend he was sorry, but as an Arab he was glad.

Our hero was stunned! He now realized that if an intelligent Arab could rejoice at his expulsion, what would uneducated, uninformed Arabs do to the small number of Jews in Palestine? Now David knew. He had no choice, he was going to America, but he would return to Palestine – destiny demanded it. His people required it!

When our hero David arrived in the United States in May 1915, he absorbed the energy of his new home. "I always dreamed of America," he wrote, "its vigorous, ultramodern life – if we want to build a new country in the desert, to raise our ruins, we must see how exiles persecuted by England constructed a state so rich, with unequaled power."

David soon joined a pioneer movement known as Hechalutz ("the pioneer"), determined to support this cause in any way possible. He began speaking in many American cities but quickly became disillusioned by the apathy of his American audiences. He was frustrated at this turn of events and decided to write a Yiddish-language adventure book about Eretz Israel. His friend Ben-Zvi was chosen to be the editor, rather than David, but in the end the book *Yizkor* (Remembrance) became a bestseller. And when his friend moved to Washington, DC, David was besieged with speaking offers: the friend was alone in the spotlight. Then, when he published a new, enlarged version of *Yizkor* on his own – soon after the first edition – it became an even bigger bestseller!

So David was becoming famous all over the world and he began to relax a little. When he finally unwound in New York, he became lonely. He pined for Rachel, and one night, while on a picnic at Coney Island, he wrote to her: "I stare into the sky and count the stars, or at the crowds on the beach, but I feel no joy – you are not here." He pleaded for her to come to America with her two children and even promised to pay her expenses. David would not receive a response. Brooding, he gave up – this wound in his soul was going to be healed – and he put an end to sentiment of a reunion with Rachel. He had lost his mother, was separated from his family, had lost his boyhood friends – now this last rejection was too much for our messiah on a mission. There was no one to talk to, no one to bare his soul to – he needed companionship more than ever at this time. What road would lead him to some happiness?

David was fortunate – very fortunate: he soon met a woman, Paula Munweis, who had just broken up with a Zionist leader. Although our hero was not as handsome or dashing as her former beau, Paula told her friend, "His appearance was bleary-eyed and shabby, but as soon as he opened his mouth, I saw that this was a great man!" David embraced his newfound friend (he had little time to waste). He desperately needed emotional nourishment from Paula, and he got it from her!

The course of David Ben-Gurion's life was now further shaped by an event that occurred on November 2, 1917. Great Britain's foreign minister, Arthur Balfour, sent Lord Rothschild, the head of the Rothschild family of Britain, a letter (known today as the Balfour Declaration) stating that "His Majesty's government views with favour the establishment in Palestine of a national home for the Jewish people, and will use their best endeavours to facilitate the achievement of this object." David was certainly elated at this news, but he was also disturbed by the euphoria and optimism permeating the Jewish world. He wrote: "England has not given us the land, it has done much by recognizing our political existence and our rights, the Hebrew people must – through labor and capital – build its national home and realize its full emancipation."

Now David had to act. Decisions had to be made. He knew he had to go to Palestine, but could he leave Paula behind without marrying her? He might lose her forever. So on December 5, 1917, David and Paula were married at a municipal building near New York City Hall. David kissed his bride, and then glanced at his watch – he was going to be late for an executive meeting of Hechalutz. He arrived late, and after explaining the reason was congratulated heartily by his colleagues. Quite a wedding reception!

David and Paula did not have a honeymoon, for he would be continuously busy – collecting money, working on his new book, or trying to get back to Palestine. Another dilemma arose at this point, complicating David's life – Paula was now pregnant with their first child. He was going to be a father! But at the same time, he heard that the British had agreed to form a Jewish Legion to fight in Palestine, a Jewish force that could eventually be used to finalize the Balfour Declaration. David's efforts had paid off, but now what could he do? If he went away to fight and was killed in battle, he would be leaving a wife – a new mother – and his child alone, forever! If this wasn't the supreme test, the measure of his commitment to a Jewish state, then what was? He had married Paula and could have easily stayed with her. Now, all over again, he made up his mind. He had to go – the Jewish state was his mission, his calling. His destiny!

David now left for training as a Jewish Legionnaire in Windsor, Canada. Training became boring and tedious, but he persevered, and in July 1918 he shipped out to England. From there, his battalion was sent to Egypt for encampment. He was very frustrated – he was so close to returning to Palestine! Finally, in November 1918, he found out he was finally going to visit.

The reason for these visits was that even though he was stationed in Egypt, Jewish leaders wanted David to attend labor meetings in Palestine, so they arranged for him to get frequent passes. David wanted to set up a powerful Hebrew labor union that would be the embryo of a Jewish state that would spare millions of Jews a miserable existence. Finally, in late 1919, a single new Labor Party was formed – Ahdut Ha'avodah (Labor Union). David was elated; he had been the instrument, the moving force that led the party.

All David needed to share this joy was his wife and his new baby girl, Geula, by his side. Finally, in November 1919, David got the British to allow his family to make the journey to Palestine. When they arrived in Jaffa, he was overwhelmed to see them. They kissed and embraced, and when he held his daughter in his arms, his yearning was fulfilled. He was grateful to his wife for her sacrifices, and his mind was now purged of guilt. His mission would now be his entire focus, totally.

Ben-Gurion's life changed again in 1921. Most Jewish workers had joined hands to form a Hebrew workers' federation called the Histadrut. He immediately recognized that his party – Ahdut Ha'avodah – must act, must be a force to join with and then control this new federation, the Histadrut. He believed that, politically, the labor movement would be a force that would create new jobs, spawning and generating new industries, companies, mines, banks, and even socialized medicine!

David was elected and served as general secretary of the Histadrut from 1921 until 1925. In time, the Histadrut indeed became the dominating influence on the land's economy, politics, social institutions, factories, and banks. The party went into the construction field as well to create jobs for new immigrants, who were excluded from British and Arab projects. Finally, in May 1930, as the Histadrut's powers expanded under Ben-Gurion, the two largest political parties were merged to form the Mapai party.

While all these amazing progressions were occurring in David's quest for a state, his family remained in the background. His three children saw little of their father, who came and went like a ghost. His son, Amos, then a young boy, understood his father even though he never got presents from him. "I respected him and looked up to him – that was enough for me," Amos later said. Once, when Amos misbehaved, his father greeted him with, "Amos, when I am old, the one thing I'll regret is I didn't pay enough attention to you – but I have a mission to perform and I cannot divide my attention. Please, Amos, realize the burden that I shall feel when I'm old." Amos became upset that he had caused his father uneasiness, and replied, "Don't worry, Father, I'll find my way, you go ahead with your mission!" His young son, even at age ten, knew his father and understood his need for study and focus.

David pressed on despite family challenges and pressures. But events now took place that placed a cloud over our hero's ambitions for a Jewish state. First, in 1919, the Arab mufti of Jerusalem, uneasy over the growth of the Jewish population, decided to act against the Jews. Arab leaders soon began to instigate random attacks, which grew into organized riots; hundreds of Jews and Arabs were killed. The Arabs wanted to reduce Jewish immigration and weaken the intentions of the Balfour Declaration. These terrible riots did produce some positive results for the Jewish settlers, however: first, our hero David now considered the Haganah an underground defense force, free of foreign (British) control; secondly, David now realized Britain could not be counted on to protect Jews in Palestine.

Years later, in 1929, after David returned from the Sixteenth Zionist Congress in Zurich, he had to confront another serious problem. He realized that the Arab frenzy of continuous riots and violence had to be addressed – addressed and resolved. David wanted ten thousand new Jewish immigrants, an expanded Haganah, and a Jewish police force in every Jewish town! Violence to meet violence! This was met by the "Passfield White Paper" of 1930, in which the British stated that only a limited number of Jews could set foot in Palestine. Our hero was furious. He even took to the street, saying, "No White Paper – we will determine our own destiny – we must resist!" His comrades were not convinced. "Fight the British Empire?" they said. David had frightened many Zionists with his words, but those who knew him understood that his real strategy was to scare his enemies!

The years after 1930 saw our hero's life, and his political strategy to conquer the whole Zionist movement, take shape. He needed to over-come the leadership of Chaim Weizmann and the "right-wing" Ze'ev

Jabotinsky; David believed Weizmann had been too soft, too willing to compromise on a Jewish state, where Jews would not be the majority. Eventually, Weizmann would be nudged out of his leadership role as president of the WZO. Soon after that, Jabotinsky's hard-line proposals were rejected as well, as too radical, too far-right – "a state at any cost, now," was his mantra.

Finally, on August 25, 1933, as David Ben-Gurion stepped to the rostrum of the WZO in Prague, he was met with tumultuous applause. Dressed in a crumpled gray suit and open-collared white shirt, he began to realize that he had stumbled to the summit of world Zionism. He still faced opposition from Jabotinsky's Revisionist Party, however. They wanted a Jewish state immediately, and our David knew that a state would take some time. "First, fill up the country with Jews; create power, and then demand a state," he repeated for all to hear.

In 1935, at the Nineteenth World Zionist Congress, David was faced with choices. Beseeched by his party to be "prime minister" of a shadow government, he balked. Chaim Weizmann would return as president, knowing all the while that our hero David would be the real power in the WZO.

In April 1936, a chain reaction of events was triggered. Two Jews were killed on a road near Nablus, without any warning. Then Arab bands in Jaffa knifed and shot sixteen Jews to death. Street crimes? An organized rebellion? After the Arabs began a general strike on April 22, closing down shops, factories, and ports, they demanded of the British that Jewish immigration be completely stopped! But David saw this as an opportunity. He ordered the Haganah to uncase their rifles, but only to defend themselves – they were to be guided by one concept: *havlagah* (restraint). David believed that "terrorism benefits the Arabs. We cannot be blind to the gulf between us." He realized that British sympathy for the Jewish cause would trump any violence between the Arabs and the Jews.

He spoke to the Royal Commission in Britain in January 1937, offering a compromise: Palestine did not have to be a separate Jewish state, but could it exist as a member of a greater unit? He was in essence saying that a Jewish state was unnecessary at that time! No one believed it of the Zionist leader. But the Commission's reaction was unprecedented. It recommended terminating the mandate and splitting Palestine into an independent Jewish state and an independent Arab state. Our hero was stunned, amazed. Britain was now speaking of a Jewish state, and so was he! They were on the same page – finally!

The Arabs rejected this solution completely, of course. They did not want a Jewish homeland or Jewish immigration. Even the WZO opposed the plan, as they thought the new state would be too small. More Arab uprisings that year led to hundreds of deaths in Palestine. Finally, after two years of British commissions studying the situation, a conference was called in London in February 1939 that ended in failure, with the Arabs refusing to enter into any agreement that allowed Jewish immigration. David was livid, and challenged the British immediately. "Jews cannot be prevented from immigrating into the country except by force of British bayonets, police, and navy," he objected, "and Palestine cannot be an Arab state over Jewish opposition and without the help of British bayonets!" The British were shocked – how very un-Jewish. But David knew that British public opinion was on their side; they would not stand for barbarism!

In the wake of the 1939 White Paper restricting Jewish immigration, and allowing an Arab Palestinian state, David made plans for a Jewish resistance. He became the head of the Jewish Agency and assumed command of the Haganah, becoming, in essence, defense minister of the Zionist movement. He began by ordering immediate Jewish immigration despite its illegality under the White Paper. His actions were rebuffed by a majority of his colleagues, however. He was certainly dismayed at this turn of events.

The war years of the 1940s were difficult for our hero. He came to America in 1942 to define the aims of Zionism. At a conference in New York City in May 1942, he enthralled the six hundred delegates with his new solution – scrap the White Paper, form a Jewish army and a Jewish immigration committee, and continue Jewish immigration and settlement. This proposal, called the Biltmore Program after the hotel in which this meeting took place, was approved by a majority of representatives. Our David carried the day, with Chaim Weizmann and others in attendance. He now felt upbeat about moving forward with his agenda.

Sadly, this was followed by the news of his father's death – Avigdor had died, he read in a cable with tears in his eyes. His father, David remembered, had been to many meetings where David had spoken, beaming, his eyes aglow. He was so proud of his son. David wrote Paula at the time, "I inherited from him my love for the Jewish people, Eretz Israel, the Hebrew language. He was a rare father – full of love." He would miss him terribly in the years to come.

World War II was a pall over the world, and certainly over the Jews of Europe. After German troops had invaded Poland in 1939, David Ben-Gurion, in spite of great differences with Great Britain, said, "We shall fight the war as if there is no White Paper," and "This is our war no less than Britain's or Russia's war!" The Jews of Palestine then made a great contribution to the British cause: 130,000 Jews registered as volunteers for military service in the first month of the war. By the war's end, thirty-two thousand were on active duty with British forces and had fought in some of the fiercest campaigns. The British War Cabinet had also sanctioned the creation of a Jewish Brigade of five thousand volunteers from Palestine, flying the yellow Star of David, against Arab objections, of course. They fought the German army valiantly in Italy and were highly regarded by the British command.

But while the war was still in progress and Germany was taking control of Europe, word leaked to Palestine and its leaders, of Nazi atrocities against the Jews of Europe. The reports were at first deemed "doubtful and unreliable" and were treated "with caution and suspicion." But then additional reports from survivors corroborated the stories of mass Jewish slaughter by the Nazi regime. David blasted the Allies for their passive attitude. "What have you allowed to be perpetrated against a defenseless people, while you step aside without calling on the friends to stop in the language of retribution – they would understand?" He then challenged the Allies to allow the Jews to "take up arms against the Nazis as a nation of Jews in a Jewish army under a Jewish flag!"

Although David did lament the Holocaust as it was unfolding, he kept his focus on the emerging Jewish state. He feared that pressing the Allies too hard on the issue would jeopardize his chances of creating a Jewish army, and then a Jewish state. He did mention that Pope Pius XII could have spoken out against the annihilation of Jews, could have denounced it, and that the Pope's voice would have resonated. David's voice would have been a squeak in comparison. Although our David bemoaned the plight of the Jews in Europe and was horrified by the unfolding tragedy, he still could not permit sentiment and the unbearable guilt to influence his priorities and steer him away from his messianic course. He would continue on his mission. His awareness of the reports from Europe certainly contributed to his impassioned plea for Jewish immigration at the Biltmore conference.

During the war years, politics dominated our hero's time, and his family suffered for it. He was away a great deal, and even when he was home he was constantly attending meetings. Paula rarely saw our hero, and the children had grown up. Once, to his daughter Renana, with whom he shared an apartment in Jerusalem, he casually and callously remarked, "You're not very pretty, how did you get all those boyfriends?" This young and attractive woman knew her father. She understood his priorities, his thinking – she didn't need compliments from him. She loved him anyway, for what he was and who he was.

On May 8, 1945, Germany finally surrendered to the Allies. The war in Europe was over, but our hero was sad, very sad. The world, he thought, was savoring the new peace (Japan was to collapse soon too). But would the world forget the Jewish people? The Jews needed to fight a final battle, and David was going to lead it! He flew to London to appeal to the British: "Reject the White Paper and permit a million Jews into Palestine," he demanded. He was denied by Winston Churchill, who wanted to wait for the Allies to sit down at the peace table. Even President Franklin Roosevelt, who claimed he supported Zionism, had demanded they stand down. David now turned back to the United States – to American Jews – who would politically and financially join his fight and use their power in a last battle for a Jewish state.

In reality David knew that when the British left Palestine, the Arab armies would try to destroy the Yishuv (the Jewish settlement in Eretz Israel). He also knew he needed money to buy arms and weapons to equip the Haganah in this fight. The call for help to wealthy American Jews was answered by Rudolf Sonneborn, an industrialist, who knew his associates, and others, would also meet the challenge. They formed the Sonneborn Institute in order to buy tons of government surplus arms and ships from any source available – including the mafia! Even American Jewish veterans participated, leaving souvenir firearms at "gun drops." After all this, our hero sent a letter to Moshe Sneh, the Haganah chief in Palestine, ordering to begin an Aliyah Gimmel – an armed uprising. They would rush refugee immigrants into Eretz Israel to commit acts of sabotage and retaliation (but with no intentional fatalities) – the time had come for action!

Our hero stopped in Frankfurt, Germany, on October 19, 1945, and went to a displaced persons camp in Zeilsheim. The crowd was large and boisterous – they shouted, "Ben-Gurion!" David stood on a platform, looked over the crowd, and choked up. His eyes watered – he was filled with emotion! There was muffled sobbing from all parts of the hall. "Zion is waiting for you," he said. "Patience, you will leave soon!" The crowd listened and trusted and loved our hero. They believed in his leadership in their homeland-to-be, that they would be delivered.

Before leaving Germany, David stopped at Allied headquarters and saw American general Dwight Eisenhower, whom he asked for help in settling refugees in Palestine. The general wanted to help when Ben-Gurion suggested a weekly air shuttle to Palestine, but was denied when Washington backed off under British pressure, a too-familiar occurrence in those days.

David was not dismayed. He had viewed the gas chambers where millions of his fellow Jews had perished, and he now believed the Holocaust had turned survivors into fanatical Zionists – they all longed for Eretz Israel!

Soon the Haganah joined with the militant Irgun and the radical Lechi (the Stern gang) to launch a Hebrew Resistance movement in Palestine. Daring operations freed illegal immigrants in the Atlit detention camp, sabotaged railroads, bridges, and supplies and blew up British Coast Guard ships. The British were totally shocked. Britain's parliament decided to set up a commission of Americans and Britons to decide where Jewish refugees should settle; when the commission issued a report in favor of discontinuing the policies of the White Paper and calling for the immediate entry of 100,000 Jewish refugees, Foreign Secretary Ernest Bevin turned it down flat!

David reacted quickly to this broken promise. The Aliyah Gimel was begun anew, with the Haganah destroying bridges, roads, and railroads. The British, however, in retaliation, on June 29, 1946, instigated what came to be called "Black Saturday," declaring a general curfew in the entire Yishuv to intimidate the population and to flush out the Jewish paramilitary once and for all. Thousands of arrests were made. The situation was becoming critical – David, our hero, knew that practically the entire Jewish leadership in Palestine was behind barbed wire! What could he do at this desperate moment? Things looked hopeless and bleak under his leadership.

David decided that then, at that point in time, it was time for a Jewish state. He sought international support from Vietnam and other countries, but returned to the United States to acquire more funds for arms and ships. He knew that the British must go, so while in New York he approved a daring act– to blow up the King David Hotel! The King David Hotel was at the time the site of the British military command and Central Intelligence Division. The united Hebrew Resistance believed that the truckloads of their sensitive documents that had been seized during "Black Saturday" were stored in the hotel.

David quickly changed his mind, remembering *havlagah* (restraint); the cost would be too high, he knew. But fate had other plans, for the Irgun leader Menachem Begin did not agree to restrain. He would have his men do it, with or without Haganah approval, and he did, killing nearly one hundred people with the blast!

Ben-Gurion was condemned by all, including the liberal newspaper *Ha'aretz*, which demanded his resignation. These Jewish bombs had split the Yishuv and threatened the very existence of the Zionist movement. David was now forced into a position of moderation – he had to align himself with his old nemesis, Chaim Weizmann, to achieve credibility once again. David nominated Weizmann as president of the WZO – a position with honor, but no power. Weizmann rejected the nomination, but when he challenged David's leadership, no one listened. David Ben-Gurion now stood alone, once again, at the pinnacle of the Zionist movement.

So our hero was at a crossroads. What to do about the plight of Palestine? David knew that the "Black Saturday" tactic had failed the British – the Jewish terrorists in Palestine were on a rampage, which pressured the British to release the Jewish prisoners they held. Bevin now met with David in London to discuss options. A four-year British trusteeship, followed by Jewish and Arab independence, was turned down by David. Finally, alone with Secretary Bevin, he asked what Bevin's needs and fears were in Palestine. But before he got an answer, David blurted out, "Is it possible to find a solution that will satisfy us both?" Bevin then made a momentous pronouncement – he would let the United Nations determine Palestine's future; the meeting ended.

It was now obvious to David that the cost, in terms of prestige as well as funds needed to support British troops in Palestine, was too high for the British to bear. David now knew that whatever the UN decided, the British would soon be out of Palestine, and the Arabs would be coming in. He therefore mobilized the Haganah as a conventional army capable of striking with speed and mobility. They needed twelve infantry brigades, three armored brigades, as many aircraft as they could get, and 120,000 rifles, if possible. David was determined to save the Yishuv from imminent danger. New arms shipments were now being rushed to Palestine, and illegal immigration was sped up as well, as it had been since the end of World War II, to fuel the birth of a Jewish state. Sixty ships, carrying 100,000 refugees, would sail the Mediterranean to the Promised Land. Not all would get through the British fleet, however.

In June 1947, the United Nations Special Committee on Palestine (UNSCOP) flew to the Holy Land to determine the claims of both Jews and Arabs. David addressed them: "Who is willing and capable of guaranteeing that what happened to us in Europe will not recur? Can the conscience of humanity absolve itself of all responsibility for that Holocaust? There is only one security guarantee – a homeland and a state!" This event took place while the maritime exodus, carrying hundreds of Jewish refugees, was being sent back to Europe by the British. Amazing! On September 3, 1947, UNSCOP issued a majority report – there would be one Arab and one Jewish state, with Jerusalem internationalized! The UN General Assembly, however, would have the final say in the matter.

Our hero now had to act, and act quickly, to ensure that the Jewish state would finally become a reality. He kept his staff at the UN working night and day to persuade delegates – particularly Americans – to the Jewish cause. He even convinced his old nemesis, Chaim Weizmann, to see President Harry Truman and gain his support for a Jewish state covering the full territory of the mandate. David needed two thirds of the General Assembly for final approval of partition, and he needed King Abdullah of Jordan to side with him. Golda Meir was sent to meet with the Jordanian king in Amman, where he agreed to their mutual needs – Jordan would absorb the Palestinian Arab state and prevent Arab armies from attacking the new Jewish state! Very good news.

All was now ready. Our advocate had been unrelenting in his drive for statehood – was the moment finally here? On November 29, 1947, David was fast asleep in a hotel on the Dead Sea, exhausted by his efforts. The door burst open, and a messenger from the Jewish Agency in Jerusalem burst into the room. "Mazel tov!" he cried out. "We won!"

David Ben-Gurion was overwhelmed with joy. He immediately got up and wrote these words:

> The Jewish people…will not fall short at this great hour of opportunity and the historic responsibility that has been given to it. The restored Judea will take an honorable place in the United Nations as a force for peace, prosperity, and progress in the Holy Land, the Near East, and the world at large.

The plan for partition had passed the vote in the UN General Assembly. There was dancing in the streets, but our hero knew that there would be a price to pay – an impending war with the Arabs. Certainly new problems arose – howling Arab mobs wreaked havoc in Jerusalem while the British looked on. Other incidents saw Arabs attacking Jewish settlements with reckless abandon. They ambushed Jewish convoys along the main roads to Jerusalem.

Our hero had to act – yet again. The Yishuv had to be prepared for all contingencies. Finally, after Deir Yassin (an Arab village) was attacked and decimated by Irgun and Lehi paramilitary forces, with many Arabs killed, Ben-Gurion was filled with terrible remorse. The Haganah had violated *havlagah*. What to do? David did not do anything, nor did he need to, because thousands of Arabs on donkeys soon began retreating to their Arab states. They were running away from Jewish military retaliation. The Jews were now the dominant population in Palestine. The Arabs had gone.

Other obstacles arose, including the obstruction of US Secretary of State George Marshall, who wanted to postpone the declaration of a Jewish state. Even King Abdullah wanted a delay, fearing a war looming on the horizon.

So again David was at a crossroads. Openly declare a state to the world, and endure a war? Not declare a state, and war anyway? He was torn. Finally, at a meeting of the national council, he posed the question. Approve the Marshall Plan, which would postpone the creation of a new state? Or stay the course and disapprove the

Marshall Plan to finally make his dream of a new Jewish state realty?

David knew he had to force the issue, and presented it to the National Council of Thirteen. If they declared a state now, what were the chances of success, of victory? Fifty-fifty was the answer from the head of the Haganah, Yaakov Dori. David couldn't stop now and decided to throw the dice!

The air was electric. The past – the millions of Nazi victims – and the future – the destiny of the nation – rode on this present moment.

The vote was finally taken, the truce was rejected, and the decision to declare independence was supported by six of the ten voting members!

David finally smiled broadly. Two days later, on May 14, 1948, David Ben-Gurion declared the new Jewish state to the entire world, and the rebirth of Israel, at what became Independence Hall in Tel Aviv. He spoke at this historic occasion, saying, "We had been a minority in scores of lands for almost two thousand years, our fate determined by others. We just lost six million of our people – slaughtered by the Nazis. For centuries we had been like flowers in a wood – some plucked by friendly hands, others trampled underfoot and crushed. We never could be free, live a normal life, affect our own decisions, our destiny. Now the hour has struck – we are independent once again." Our hero had achieved his calling, his mission – his destiny – in spite of overwhelming odds!

David continued to serve his people and his country as prime minister, statesman, and writer until his death in 1973 at the ripe old age of eighty-seven. Our hero had triumphed and reached his goal – he was a messiah to the new Jewish state – but at what price? He had given up the love of his life, Rachel, for his dream. He had treated Paula as chattel, not as a wife, for most of their marriage. He did not cry at Paula's funeral when she died in 1968, but when he visited her grave a year later, he was overcome with guilt and wept. She had protected him, shared his suffering, and, most importantly, accepted his neglect. For years after her death, he would get up from the dinner table and say, "Come, Paula, let's go," not realizing she was gone forever from his life.

Our hero's spirit began to wither, but at the same time he experienced an emotional liberation by modifying the values he had held for so long. He began to mellow, finally, into a docile old man. He became more sentimental and human, reported his friends. But he had grieved more than he would ever admit. He had paid a terrible price for his devotion to Israel, the Jewish homeland. He had neglected a loving family with devoted children – what higher price could any man endure? But he had persevered, and today the State of Israel stands strong. A country of eight million inhabitants, Israel is known as a world leader in technology, venture capital start-ups, green conservation solutions, and telecommunications, and boasts a cutting-edge military – the envy of the world! David Ben-Gurion was an incredible Jewish hero whose accomplishments will stand the test of time.

He now rests in Kibbutz Sde Boker, his home in the Negev, with his wife Paula beside him. Eighty thousand tourists from all over the world come each year to pay their respects and honor a very great man, a man who changed the course of Jewish history forever.

10. Golda Meir
||||||||||||||||||||||||||||||||||||

Russia's infamous Catherine the Great had banished Russia's Jews in the late 1800s to the remotest and least economically important areas of her empire: Lithuania, Belorussia, the Crimea, Poland, and Bessarabia. Why? Did the majority ruling class fear the minority Jews? Was it blatant antisemitism at its ugliest? Or was it perhaps a combination of both? Regardless, 94 percent of Russian Jews were confined to the Pale. In addition, the impoverished Jewish shtetls had to endure constant outbreaks of antisemitic violence, which became as unpredictable and unavoidable as a natural disaster, such as a hurricane or a flood. They never knew when it would strike!

Kishinev, in 1903, was the hometown of Moshe Mabovitch, the father of our heroine, Golda Meir. Golda, born on May 3, 1898, was the second of three girls. Golda was only four years old when she experienced the pogrom that would inspire a generation of Zionists. An organized attack that spring, following blood libel allegations, saw savage murder, looting, and rape committed against the panicked Jewish townspeople of Kishinev by roving gangs of hate-driven fanatics. After the frenzy of violence subsided, the toll was added up: forty-nine Jews dead, 587 injured, seven hundred houses destroyed, 888 shops gutted, and two thousand Jewish families made homeless.

Golda's first memory was of her father, a failed carpenter, nailing wooden boards over the front door in anticipation of another pogrom. What a stressful way to live for a young girl and her family! Because of the pogroms, Golda knew at a very young age what it meant to be vilified, to be hated. Two incidents resonated with her all her days. The first occurred one afternoon while Golda was playing with a friend. A peasant grabbed her and her friend while they were playing, banged their heads together, and said, "That's what we'll do with the Jews." The second incident took place when Golda and her friends were building mud castles near her home. A troop of Cossacks rode by on their horses, slashing at the air with their swords and whips. Rather than veering around them, the Cossacks jumped over the frightened girls, shouting, "Death to the Jews!"

What can a young girl of five or six years do or say, when her earliest memories are of violence against her people? She would later say about her childhood, "I was always a little too cold outside and a little too empty inside."[21]

In addition to the constant terror surrounding her upbringing, Golda and her family never had enough to eat. Her older sister, Sheyna, fainted regularly at school for lack of nourishment; going without breakfast was the norm in their household. The family was locked in a perpetual struggle with no future to speak of, no future at all. What could they possibly look forward to?

The only positive part of Golda's life in Russia was the time her sister Sheyna spoke to a group of teenagers in their home about the evils of the tsar and the necessity of Jewish self-defense. After the guests left, Golda confronted her sister about the meeting and was soon taught about the evils of Tsarist Russia, the glories of socialism, and the dream of a Jewish homeland. Sheyna even pulled out a newspaper clipping about the future Jewish state and pointed to a photograph of a man with dark hair and a heavy beard, saying, "This is Theodor Herzl, our advocate." Sheyna was a rebellious daughter, who had been forbidden to participate in political activity by the girls' mother, Bluma. "We could be exiled or killed," she had admonished her eldest daughter. But Sheyna was Golda's heroine – she wanted very much to be like her, even at seven or eight years of age.

The family finally left Russia in 1906 to emigrate to the United States and pursue freedom. Milwaukee, Wisconsin, had been Golda's

---

21 This quotation and all those that follow in this chapter are noted in Elinor Burkett, *Golda* (New York: HarperCollins, 2009), unless otherwise indicated.

father's destination three years before, when he had left Russia to save money and prepare for his family's arrival. He was now called Morris and had worked occasionally as a carpenter, but when the rest of the family arrived, Bluma decided to rent a small grocery store to make ends meet. Golda's sister Sheyna, her idol, was now forced to run the store every morning and was very unhappy to be late to school every day. Golda, on the other hand, was enthralled by her new surroundings, drinking soda, eating ice cream, and seeing the big city. Golda was also happy taking in entertainment at the Jewish settlement house, where she mixed easily with other immigrants.

Golda was also doing well in school, always at the top of her class (although her teachers chided her for talking too much). At eight years old, she and her friends organized the American Young Sisters Society to raise money for needy classmates. In this role, she stood before her first audience and delivered an extemporaneous speech about poor immigrants who could not afford books. She even gained a certain measure of celebrity when the local newspaper picked up the story and featured a picture of Golda with her group. Golda had organized the group and succeeded at creating awareness for an issue close to her heart, on her own, for the very first time. A friend commented, "Golda has fire!"

Another incident during her youth demonstrated Golda's tenacity. When a Christian boy at school threw a penny at Golda's friend and ordered her to pick it up, she hesitated. The boy then mocked her, yelling, "A dirty Jew will pick up every penny!" Golda reacted, immediately, by organizing a demonstration against antisemitism right in front of the boy's house!

By now, Golda's sister Sheyna had not only worn out her welcome at home but also unfortunately contracted tuberculosis (TB) – a disease that forced her parents to send her to Denver, to a Jewish hospital there. Then, when Sheyna heard that Shamai Korngold, her old heartthrob from Russia, was coming to Milwaukee, she redirected him to Denver, where they soon married. But Golda missed her sister terribly; Sheyna was her closest friend and a faithful adviser. Golda persevered, graduating from elementary school and giving the valedictory address. (Even then, at age twelve, she was a recognized speaker!)

Golda's mother Bluma had old-fashioned visions for her daughter, ideas Golda totally disagreed with. She wanted to go to high school, and then teacher's college, and certainly take a good job someday, but her mother only wanted her to work and then "marry, marry, marry!" Her mother's ideal future for Golda was to be a mother and housekeeper; as she said, "A very clever woman you'll never be." Even her father agreed: "Men don't like smart women!" But Golda was very stubborn and prevailed over her parents' wishes, enrolling in North Division High School in 1912, when she was just fourteen years old.

She had won the battle with her parents, this time, but two months later, she rebelled! Her mother unexpectedly announced that she wanted Golda to marry a certain prosperous man – a man twice her age. To Golda, Bluma had finally crossed the line. After pouring her heart out to her sister Sheyna, Golda made a decision. She was moving to Denver, on her own, at only fourteen years of age!

Even then, Golda had a mantra. "Only those who dare, who have the courage to dream, can really accomplish anything. Others who ask, 'Is it worth trying?' accomplish nothing!"

So one night, Golda packed her bags, lowered them out the window to a waiting friend, and went back to sleep. The next day, she followed her daily routine – she ate her breakfast, took her books, said goodbye, and was, supposedly, going to school, or so her parents thought. She recovered her suitcase at her best friend's house, took a trolley to the railroad station, and bought a ticket to Denver! She spent every dime, even pennies from Sheyna and money from friends, to go to be with her sister and her sister's new husband. How many fourteen-year-old girls, in any generation, would or could do this? This was 1912, and feminism was hardly in vogue, yet Golda was liberating herself from the "tyranny and oppression" of her parents. To her, there was little struggle, no real hardship, and no risk. Soon after arriving in Denver she was sleeping in a comfortable bed in her sister Sheyna's brick bungalow, happy to be free of her parents' control.

Golda thrived in her sister's home in Denver for two years, working at Sheyna's husband's dry cleaning business, going to school, and helping with meals. She was very happy. She was also learning about the world at large: Sheyna's house frequently vibrated with discussions on many subjects. Golda listened while Zionism, women's emancipation, socialism, Leninism, and class struggle were debated. She became a very good listener, but one subject really captured her interest and imagination – Zionism. An intellectual named Aaron David Gordon, who later came to be known as the father of Labor Zionism, had written that "The Land of Israel is acquired through labor, not through fire and not blood – we must create a new human people with a sense of brotherhood – the rebirth of our people is needed." Golda was fascinated by the concept of Zionism, so she devoured every magazine she could find for information on the pioneers who would someday return to Palestine.

Sheyna, however, thought Golda was becoming too forward, too independent, at sixteen years of age. Though Golda craved her sister's approval, she was not going to give up her freedom to her sister, who was being "overly motherly" and dominating – she had already run away from that once. One night, after dinner, Sheyna berated Golda one time too many. "I'm not a baby!" Golda exploded. "You have no right to boss me around. I'm leaving!" Sheyna's response: "Go ahead!"

So Golda left, even leaving her cherished books behind, with nowhere to go. She wasn't going back to Milwaukee! She wasn't going to apologize to Sheyna! What was she to do? Golda did what she would do her whole life – she refused to give in, to compromise her principles. She was now on her own with no place to stay, so she rented an apartment by herself. She was all of sixteen years old! Talk about chutzpah!

Having said goodbye to her beloved sister, Golda was now completely alone for the first time in her life and soon became very lonely. She managed to get a job and was getting by, day to day, but she craved companionship and friendship. She had met a twenty-one-year-old man at Sheyna's house named Morris Meyerson, and one day he invited her to a free concert in the park. He was a quiet, unassuming man, with thinning hair and steel-rimmed glasses, but he began to pierce her vulnerability – the steel shield she had developed living with a tough mother and a tougher sister. Soon, they were spending considerable time together, at concerts and at various lectures on science, philosophy, and psychology. Morris became her mentor, teacher, brother, and lover! Golda later said of Morris: "He's not particularly good-looking, but he has a beautiful soul."

Fate, however, had other things in mind for Golda. Out of the blue, she got a letter from her father, who wanted her to come home. Her parents even pledged to support her in going to high school and becoming a teacher! "Please come home for your mother," he wrote.

So Golda relented. Home again in Milwaukee, she began, in addition to attending high school, to do relief work – going door to door to beg nickels for displaced Jews in Europe. World War I had started, and both sides of the conflict – Russians and Germans – were killing thousands of Jews and leaving millions more homeless. She was eventually noticed by a Labor Zionist, Isadore Tuchman, because of her activities organizing meetings and speeches to help Jews. Tuchman's movement was Workers of Zion (Po'alei Zion), whose goal was to prepare its members to move to Palestine. Golda began to see that her future was not in America, but was part of a cause: contributing to building Palestine. Unlike others of her generation, Golda was not going to be a "Parlor Zionist" – all talk and no action. She was going to dedicate her life to Zionism!

Soon, her beloved Morris moved to Milwaukee to be with her and, for a while, they both worked toward their goals – Morris as a painter, Golda studying at a teacher's college. But Golda was still not content; she wasn't happy. She yearned to go to the Holy Land; she wanted to strike a blow for Jewish independence. She could not allow herself to be docile and passive, not Golda!

Morris had dreamed of a quiet life with Golda – to raise children and a family in America, not Palestine. No way. But, when she finally gave him an ultimatum – to Palestine, or no marriage! – he had to give in to her. They were married in December 1917 in a simple, unpretentious ceremony at her parents' home. The wedding meal was boiled potatoes, herring, and sponge cake. They did, however, have a chuppah and a rabbi who performed the ceremonial prayers for the newlyweds. Golda was nineteen years of age.

In the same year, another event occurred that greatly impacted our Golda's life. The Balfour Declaration had been issued by the British government in 1917, saying it "viewed with favour" a Jewish state in Palestine. This now motivated Golda to join and support the American Jewish Congress, campaigning for Zionist delegates. She even got herself elected as a delegate to the convention. And there at the convention, she listened to prominent American Jews speak in opposition to Zionism for fear that it would cause Jews the world over to be singled out, leading to greater persecution. She rose to her feet and spoke with passion and dedication. It made an impact – "I tell you, her mouth was gold," her leader Tuchman later blurted out. She persuaded the American Jewish Congress to adopt the resolution for Palestine, with only two votes dissenting. It was then, at twenty years of age, that Golda had found her calling. She had stood up to America's most prominent Jews, and won. She wrote Morris from the convention: "I didn't miss a single session – this is the life for me." She was happy she had found her niche, her passion.

There was no stopping Golda – they were going to Palestine, and now! Golda and Morris endured a journey of fifty-three days aboard a dilapidated ship named the USS *Pocahontas*, which had broken down twice on the way. With them were Golda's sister Sheyna and Sheyna's two children. After arriving in Naples, their initial plan to board another ship to Palestine was thwarted due to Arab riots that were occurring in Jaffa. Thus, she and Morris, and seventeen other pioneers, arrived in Tel Aviv by train on July 14, 1921. The sand was ankle deep, and there were no trees to speak of. They were all in Palestine, at last.

Golda had always wanted to live on a kibbutz, building Jewish socialism. But when she and Morris applied to one – Kibbutz Merhavia in northern Palestine – they were not accepted. Golda did not give up, and although the leaders of the kibbutz disdained "soft" Americans, they had not encountered a woman of her tough dogmatism before. After three votes, she and Morris were finally accepted, on the condition that they prove themselves worthy before one month had elapsed. Golda picked almonds and planted trees, and Morris worked the fields. They persevered and were fully accepted. Morris would later say that they were approved because of his phonograph and collection of classical records!

Life on a kibbutz in Palestine at that time was primitive – ramshackle huts, a communal kitchen, and a latrine a quarter of a mile from their abode. Golda adapted to the lifestyle; whether it was swinging a pickax or running a chicken coop (she was deathly afraid of chickens!), she did it. She was doing her best to fit in, and was succeeding. Morris, however, disdained the communal lifestyle, and while Golda thrived on attending political meetings and dancing the hora, he preferred to be alone with his music.

Amazingly, after a few months, Golda was offered the opportunity to represent the kibbutz at a convention at Degania – the lodestar of Labor Zionism. She jumped at the chance. While there, she was in the presence of leading figures of the Labor Zionist cause – David Ben-Gurion, Levi Eshkol, and David Remez, to name a few.

Golda was awed into silence listening to the convention participants speaking Hebrew, the language of the pioneers. She was enthralled beyond words and went home to Morris, who had contracted malaria and was depressed. Golda was sympathetic to him, but was dedicated more than ever to continuing her progress in this important movement. She joined the Women's Workers Council, which would eventually be merged into the Histadrut, headed by none other than David Ben-Gurion. She managed to gain the attention of the leadership by speaking out against its treatment of women. Ben-Gurion was dazzled by her eloquence; soon, she was invited to tour Jewish Palestine with a British official.

When she returned from her trip, Morris had had enough of her absences, saying he wanted children and a life, and was ready to deliver an ultimatum. If she wanted to have children with him, they would have to abandon the kibbutz life. Golda's good friend Marie Syrkin would observe that Morris had become irrational and emotionally dependent on Golda's account, and that Golda's commitment to her husband was based on this troublesome dynamic. "She was bound by his bondage!" Marie later said.

Golda and Morris then moved to Tel Aviv, where she managed to work part-time as a cashier for Solel Boneh, the building cooperative of the Histadrut. Here they stayed, until, soon, a job opened up for Morris at Solel Boneh's Jerusalem branch. Golda followed him there, to be near him – he needed her desperately.

Events in Jerusalem were chaotic. Golda became pregnant, and on November 23, 1924, their son Menachem was born. But because Golda had stopped working to have her baby, their financial situation became desperate. Morris was happy in quiet, historic Jerusalem, with his dreams of a family blossoming. But Golda, on the other hand, was not happy. She felt like a prisoner, cooped up in an apartment all day long.

Golda's parents moved to Tel Aviv after arriving in Palestine in 1926, and Golda moved back to Kibbutz Merhavia with Menachem. But this only lasted a few months, because Golda was assigned child-care duties and was supremely disheartened. To her, becoming the designated "kibbutz nanny" was a frightening and degrading prospect.

Golda returned to Morris, and Jerusalem, where the couple was blessed with a daughter, Sarah, in May 1926. But things were once again very tight financially. They were about to hit rock bottom when Golda ran into an old friend, David Remez, a fellow member of the Histadrut, and a well-connected one at that. It seemed that despite all its promises, the Histadrut still had no women serving on its major policy committees, and its women's council secretary, Ada Maimon, had resigned in disgust. They were seeking to replace her with an obedient woman who would allow them to continue to control their agenda. They thought Golda was their girl!

Sadly, Golda had to move to Tel Aviv for her new job, leaving Morris behind in Jerusalem, alone. With Menachem and Sarah in tow, she was determined to make her mark in the organization. Morris kept up the facade of a marriage, showing up Saturday mornings to cook breakfast and to take the kids for walks. But Morris lived in Jerusalem during the week, and the nannies, babysitters, and kindergarten teachers were raising their children – Golda was almost never around. Golda would later admit that all her life she "felt guilty because I couldn't be the wife he wanted and should have had."

Golda plunged into her work at Histadrut headquarters. Eight years after its founding by Ben-Gurion, the Histadrut was Palestine's biggest employer, producing 33 percent of all goods in the Yishuv (Jewish settlement). The new nation was taking shape, and our heroine Golda was determined to be relevant, not just a lackey. She was then handpicked to go to America and raise money for the organization, because she had been raised in the United States and had no heavy eastern European accent, like Ben-Gurion and the others. Also, she knew how American Jews thought, both their fears and their dreams, or so she believed.

In 1928, at age thirty, Golda visited the States for the first time in seven years. She stood at the podium in front of 585 Histadrut delegates and spoke plainly and directly, talking of the Jews' struggles in Palestine, fighting Arabs and facing the British. She reached out and said, "Palestine's workers have begun a tunnel to reach their American brothers…the wall of separation is being broken down." The audience loved her candor and honesty; she was becoming the leading Histadrut emissary to the United States.

Then another opportunity arose for our Golda. There was a Labor conference in London, and Labor Zionists attended to support the socialist movement in Palestine. Ben-Gurion had spoken and had been shouted down – a very rare occurrence for him. He told Golda not to waste her breath here. But Golda never hesitated. She got to her feet and spoke to the convention with challenging words, genius, assertiveness, and sensibility. Her speech shook the convention, and Ben-Gurion was reported to have said, "I trembled at her daring words."

So Golda was now a traveling celebrity, speaking in cities all across the United States. She was also establishing herself as the only woman in the hierarchy of the Histadrut, and she never missed a meeting when in Tel Aviv. She was always dedicated and punctual.

At home, her children rarely saw their mother. Even after baby-sitters had come and gone (Golda was going to be late, again), they played and sang songs, alone, without her. Once, worried about her return, her children went to the Histadrut building and sat in the meeting room. Golda only noticed them after calling for a vote. Two of the hands raised "for" were her Menachem and Sarah's!

Sadly, Golda was never going to be a model mother in any respect; she was moving in powerful political circles, and her time for family was minimal. Her daughter Sarah said of her frequent migraines, "Even though she was sick, we were happy just to have her home." She would go away for weeks at a time, and leave behind a family who barely knew her. "The kids knew no one, no one," a family friend, Judy Goodman, reported. Another friend, Regina, put it bluntly: "Golda certainly never should have had children."

Things changed in our heroine's life beginning in the late 1930s. In 1937 Lord Peel, the British colonial administrator in Palestine, concluded at the end of his detailed investigation of the many violent disturbances in the Holy Land (which had caused more than three thousand casualties of Jews and Arabs alike) that the answer to Britain's dilemma was a partition of the country. He declared that this plan "offers a chance of ultimate peace. No other plan does."

But Golda was not happy with this compromise: the Jewish homeland would receive just one-quarter of the historical Land of Israel, with the rest cut in half. Jerusalem, Bethlehem, Galilee, and the Jezreel Valley, severed from the Jewish nation. She dismissed the partition plan as "grotesque," even when Ben-Gurion had accepted the concept as an exciting opportunity "which we never dared to dream of in our wildest imaginations." His words.

Golda was at odds with Ben-Gurion at this point. He wanted good relations with the British at all costs, whereas Golda was heavily involved in smuggling European Jews in from Poland, Austria, Romania, and Czechoslovakia. She was following her gut. "We know, we mothers," she said, "that there are Jewish children scattered everywhere in the world, and that Jewish mothers in many different countries are asking for one thing. Take our children away, take them any place you choose, only save them from this hell!" Prophetic words.

President Roosevelt called an international conference in 1938, in Lake Geneva, Switzerland, to find a solution to Hitler's expulsion and oppression of the Jews of Germany. But neither the refugees nor their envoys were given a seat at this convention! Even Chaim Weizmann was not allowed to represent the Jewish Agency. Golda too was relegated to observer status, so day after day she sat and watched as the sessions deteriorated into polite arguments. Finally, after many days of frustration, Golda had heard most of the countries' delegates make excuses for not offering refuge to help the plight of Germany's Jews. Even the United States, whose quota had been raised to 27,370 immigrants per year, was unable to help the German Jewish population until 1940. The head of Britain's delegation, Lord Winterton, stated that England was fully populated and had high unemployment.

Golda was livid. "I wanted to yell, 'Don't you know these people are human beings?'" she recalled later. At a press conference, she uttered these words: "There is one thing I want to see before I die – that my people should not heed expressions of pity anymore." Pity is all the Jews of Germany would get, to say nothing of Poland's four million and Russia's two million. Just pity was not enough for Golda. But again, what could she do?

Golda was both angry and frustrated, and went home to Tel Aviv to participate in a march of 175,000 Jews of the Yishuv, who denounced the British in one voice. It was May 1939, and the British were readying a new White Paper that was reported to impose new limits on Jewish immigration and property ownership. Eventually, after ten years of hard lobbying efforts, they would allow the creation of a state of Palestine – but not a Jewish state! Even the British Labor Party was irate at this, calling it "another victory for Hitler and Mussolini."

Golda suffered both depression and terror at this news, which endured for nine long months! How could this have happened? "It is the darkest hour of Jewish history that the British propose to deprive Jews of their last hope and close the road back to their homeland," was the Yishuv response, which Golda helped write. She now supported Ben-Gurion in building an arms industry and reorganizing the Haganah. They were also going to supply armed escorts to guarantee the safety of refugee landings. They were going to act, to respond.

The British, at this point, were distrustful of both Jews and Arabs – the Jews were defying them openly, but the Arabs had aligned themselves with the Nazis – the grand mufti was secretly receiving both money and supplies from Germany.

Golda was now at the center of the Jewish smuggling network; her apartment in Jerusalem became part of the radio network for immigrants evading the British. In addition, she was the head of austerity and rationing in Palestine, as well as mediating labor disputes at Histadrut. She even traveled throughout the Yishuv to rally support for a new tax to fund the Haganah.

She was also trying at this time to maintain a working relationship with the hated British, even though the Jewish people had been betrayed by them again and again. She balanced her true feelings by both being cordial to British officers (when necessary) and mocking them at times, saying, "They fight like lions against the Germans and Italians, but they won't stand up to the Arabs." Later she would also say, "Britain is trying to prevent the growth…of the Jewish community in Palestine, But it should remember that Jews were here two thousand years before the British came."

Why were these events occurring? The war was dragging on in Europe in 1941 and 1942, and Jews outside of Europe, including Golda, were beginning to hear news of the mass slaughter of Jews by the Nazis. In a forest near Riga, Latvia, thirty-five thousand Jews were murdered in cold blood in 1942 and nineteen thousand more were burned alive by Romanian and German troops in Odessa. Golda and her fellow Histadrut members at first refused to believe these horrible crimes were happening to their sisters and brothers in Europe. Golda desperately wanted to open a line of communication to the Jews there.

She tried making contacts with underground Jewish groups, without success. Their sense of helplessness in the face of these atrocities was excruciating for all in the Yishuv. Finally, they heard word of the Warsaw ghetto uprising – after 300,000 of their fellow ghetto residents had been sent to Treblinka for extermination. The Warsaw Jews had begun to fight the Germans – 750 brave Jews against two thousand well-armed German troops! The story of Masada came to Golda's mind, but she could not give them advice on what to do – "How can we in Tel Aviv tell them to die?" she screamed in frustration. It was not a good time in the Yishuv.

Golda had all she could do to remain sane and focused during the years of World War II. She even tried to get the British to allow the Haganah to parachute behind enemy lines, to help POWs escape and sabotage chosen targets, but the British refused, allowing only a token force.

Our heroine Golda felt helpless, and grew exhausted from her efforts – even suffering debilitating migraine headaches once again – but she persevered. She always tried to do something, no matter how small. She never quit, she never gave up. Her heart ached, but what could she do?

Finally, the agony of waiting was through. Germany surrendered in May 1945, and the war in Europe was over, but Golda knew that although millions of her Jewish brethren had died, 600,000 remained in displaced persons camps. They must be brought home, to Palestine!

Golda and other Jewish leaders were now hopeful that the British Labor Party, recently elected into power, would open the doors of Palestine to Jewish survivors of the Holocaust. But the new British policy paper merely reiterated previous attitudes regarding the Jews' and Arabs' claims – no new ground would be broken. This latest British betrayal stung the Yishuv to the core. While Britain stayed its White Paper course, news of concentration camps and mass graves was being printed in newspapers around the world. This betrayal of Zionism would not, however, be condoned by the new American president, Harry S. Truman, who indicated that "the American people, as a whole, firmly believe that immigration into Palestine should not be closed."[22] This statement by President Truman was countered by the US State Department's sympathies for Arab interests. Truman then called for the formation of a commission to investigate the Palestinian immigration issues.

Golda knew Britain's approach was intended as a stalling measure, and although she advocated *havlagah* (restraint), she did not object when the Haganah staged an uprising together with the Irgun and Lechi (the Stern gang), carrying out acts of sabotage and guerrilla attacks on British targets. This culminated in the killing of Lord Moyne, a British minister in the Middle East, by Lechi. Our heroine became the toughest hard-liner in the Histadrut hierarchy, saying, "We have to…[kill] a few boys.… [It is they who] bring catastrophe on us, not only on the British officers. Therefore, everything is permissible when it comes to them!" Quite a statement from Golda, a leader who had once worried about the British response to violence.

Golda firmly believed that "in a war for Jewish existence, every road must be an option. No road is unethical because there is nothing more ethical than helping those who survived the Holocaust to remain alive." She was continually frustrated with British reluctance to allow Jewish immigration and their resistance to a Jewish homeland. She stopped trying to sweet-talk them, wondering for the thousandth time how they could be so callous to the Jewish plight.

Finally, in March 1946, the Anglo-American Commission convened in Jerusalem. Golda talked Ben-Gurion out of his resistance to the investigation, saying that the Yishuv needed the Americans on their side. The session dragged on for hours, the members seemingly bored, when Golda took up the cause: "Many millions of Jews believe now that the only solution for the senselessness of Jewish life and Jewish death lay in creating an independent Jewish life in a Jewish homeland.

---

22 Harry S. Truman, "Letter to Attlee Concerning Resettlement of Jewish Refugees in Palestine," November 13, 1945, Jewish Virtual Library, http://www.jewishvirtuallibrary.org/president-truman-letter-to-attlee-concerning-resettlement-of-jewish-refugees-in-palestine-november-1945.

We only want what is given naturally to all peoples of this world – born free, free of fear." Her words resonated with the audience.

What followed this great speech was once again unpredictable chaos. Ultimately, the commission called for a binational state between Arabs and Jews, and, among other suggestions, the issuance of 100,000 visas for Jewish immigration into Palestine. It stressed that Great Britain's obligation to the Jews was no stronger than its obligation to the Arabs – violating the earlier pledge in the Balfour Declaration. So again, on June 17, the Jewish resistance erupted in anger over this defiance of their wishes. All the Jewish underground groups united in their resolve to use violence to fight back. On what is known as the Night of the Bridges, the Haganah blew up every road and rail bridge from Palestine to its bordering countries. The British responded with a curfew and suspension of all civil rights – "Black Saturday," as the day became known – and arrested hundreds of kibbutz residents, confiscated guns and weapons, and even arrested Yishuv leaders. Golda Meir was spared in the roundup – the British felt that she was not only a woman, but a moderating political figure, so why bother?

The "Black Saturday" weighed heavily on Golda. She had no comrades, no associates, to turn to for advice and counsel. Ben-Gurion was in Paris; Weizmann was old and sick; it was now Golda's turn to lead the Yishuv through the crisis. Newspapers decried her leadership, saying that this was not a position for a woman! They felt that Golda was a blunt force – emotional, one who only saw black and white. Many Zionist leaders were horrified by this Jewish violence and wanted to put a stop to the resistance and negotiate with the British. Golda stood tall and declared to the Yishuv that they wanted total independence. Golda stood strong at first, but was soon worn down by prodding from her old boss, David Remez, who recommended she invoke a peaceful solution. She began speaking out in favor of dialing down the violence of the resistance, of fighting for independence with civil disobedience. But to her dismay, the Haganah wasn't listening. They continued their alliance with the other Jewish underground groups and collaborated to plan the single deadliest terror attack in Palestine's history. On

July 22, 1946, the Irgun bombed Jerusalem's King David Hotel, where British military and intelligence were headquartered, killing ninety-one people and wounding hundreds. Even Jewish leaders were fighting amongst themselves at this point – Ben-Gurion wanted to negotiate with the British, as did Weizmann and Remez. Remez chastised Golda for "destroying the last hope of the Jewish people."

Golda was now suffering gallstones and frequent migraine headaches. She was taking semi-regular morphine injections, which left her worn down.

Jewish survivors in DP camps in Europe were going to have to endure another cold winter. Some countries were still under martial law. Despite all the cautious diplomacy and not-so-cautious resistance, the Yishuv was still floundering.

At a Zionist conference in Basel, Switzerland, in late 1946, Golda and Ben-Gurion butted heads again. President Truman had a clear goal in mind, a Jewish state with its size and shape specified. Ben-Gurion announced that he would compromise and accept a partitioning of the mandate into two states, but Golda insisted on the bold declaration of a Jewish state covering the mandate's full territory. "If Truman really is prepared to offer us a State of Israel, then let's request it now!"

Now, finally, Britain's Prime Minister Clement Attlee, under unrelenting pressure from Harry Truman, against the backdrop of a British public tired of their media detailing violence and executions in Palestine, announced he would submit the question of Palestine to the newly formed United Nations!

In the fall of 1947, our heroine Golda disguised herself as an Arab woman and traveled to Amman, Jordan, to undertake delicate political negotiations with King Abdullah. Golda and the Yishuv needed the king to agree to not send his Arab Legion against the soon-to-be-established Jewish state. And even though the king dreamed of an empire including Syria, Lebanon, and Palestine, his greatest threat was not the Yishuv, but al-Husseini, the former mufti of Jerusalem, who also had his own expansionist dreams in the area. So, since the Jews hated al-Husseini even more than King Abdullah did, the

Zionists were going to be his allies! Interesting logic at a crucial time in Jewish history.

Golda's visit to the king was hardly expected – a woman in a conservative Arab world could not be the equal of men, certainly not in politics, or so went the thought. Regardless, he spoke to her with respect. Even better, her translators believed the king's responses indicated his intention not to conspire with his ethnic brethren in a war with the new Jewish state. However, Golda wondered how reliable that promise would be in the near future, unsure if the king's word would be kept indefinitely.

Golda was soon busy with other matters in 1947, including bringing to Palestine Jewish children who were living in British detention centers on the island of Cyprus. She finally got the parents of the children to agree to allow them to leave alone. It was agonizing for Golda, who went to the British commander for permission, which was granted – Golda won the day.

The United Nations was set to vote on a plan of partition of the Palestine Mandate, with an internationalized Jerusalem. No one in the Yishuv was sure that the necessary two-thirds majority would be reached. But on November 29, 1947, the final vote showed thirty-three nations for, thirteen against, and ten abstentions. Great Britain was one of the abstentions, to no one's great surprise. The next day, in Jerusalem, with Star of David flags fluttering, Golda stood next to David Ben-Gurion on the balcony of the Jewish Agency building and spoke: "For two thousand years we have waited – we always believed it would come.… Now we shall have a free Jewish state."

Golda's work was not over with this great news. The Yishuv now needed weapons and equipment to ensure its survival against the inevitable Arab onslaught. Golda was told that the Jews of Palestine could only be counted on for $7 or $8 million for this effort. She was also told that American Jews were tapped out, but that millions more were needed. Ben-Gurion wanted to take on this challenge – go to the States and raise money – but Golda intervened, saying, "What you can do here, I cannot do – but what you can do in the United States, I can also do." Golda had her way, and was soon on her way to the United States with a shopping list! Weapons, ammunition, blankets, tents, and sweaters were all needed to prepare the newly formed state for its impending struggle.

Golda arrived in the United States in early January 1947, and was welcomed not only by the worst blizzard in fifty years, but the director of the United Jewish Appeal as well. Executive Vice President Henry Montor considered her an unimportant representative – a "schnorrer" (huckster) for various small funds. She did not get a very warm reception; Montor was more interested in protecting his own charity – his own investors – than in purchasing weapons for the Yishuv.

Every other major American Jewish organization was also opposed to Golda's efforts, but she was undaunted. Montor directed her to Chicago and the Council of Federations and Welfare Funds, one of the largest Jewish charities in the country at that time. What happened in Chicago? At first, they refused her the opportunity to speak – but Montor mounted pressure, and a thankful Golda was finally allowed to address the council at a Sunday luncheon where the *baalei batim* (the rich guys) would be in attendance!

Eight hundred wealthy Texan Jews were gathered in the Sheraton hotel that day – rich, cynical, and hard-nosed – not Golda's people. She was very plainly dressed, in a simple blue outfit, with her hair pulled back tightly in a bun. Golda was facing one of the great challenges of her life – she was going to address a mostly non-Zionist crowd, a group not really sympathetic to Yiddish-speaking socialists in any shape or form. She had arrived days earlier, in a blizzard, without even enough money to pay for a cab. Now she was on her way to speak to one of the wealthiest groups of Jewish businessmen in the world!

Golda spoke off the cuff in her direct, no-nonsense manner. She talked of the UN resolution enabling the establishment of a Jewish state in Palestine, and how the Jews of that state now had to fight for their lives, for their safety, and, most importantly, for Jewish honor and independence. She continued: "If we have arms to fight with, we will fight with those, and if not, we will fight with stones in our hands."

She added that where the grand mufti had Arab states with budgets to rely on, the Yishuv had millions of Jews in the Diaspora, and they had faith in Jews in the United States. She ended her speech by saying, "You cannot decide whether we should fight or not. We will. You can only decide one thing – whether we shall be victorious in this fight or whether the mufti will be victorious. That decision…has to be made quickly, within hours, within days. And I beg of you – don't be too late. Don't be bitterly sorry three months from now for what you failed to do today. The time is now!"

Montor, her guide, commented after her speech that she had electrified the crowd – these non-Zionists from Texas were going to raise so much money, they wouldn't know what to do with it! Golda had carried the day, brilliantly.

Even Miami, with all its glitz, was taken with Golda. She raised five million dollars there in just one day! Finally, the UJA agreed to include Golda's request in their campaign, since she had raised $25 million on her own in less than two months. In her last speech, in New York, she was stark and blunt: "Do you want a Jewish state we can celebrate in Madison Square Garden, or another memorial meeting for Jews in Palestine who are gone?"

Her trip was over at last; Golda Meir had raised a total of $50 million for the Haganah, for Jewish survival! Ben-Gurion lauded her, calling her the "Jewish woman who got the money which made the state possible."[23]

Back in Palestine, Golda worked non-stop, even suffering a mild heart attack in mid-April. Ben-Gurion needed her to placate King Abdullah, who was wavering in his agreement to avoid war with the new Jewish state. The British, whose military had yet to pull out of the territory, had agreed to allow the king free rein to take on all of Palestine (after a Jewish defeat, of course)! Our good friends the British were still at it! Golda did see the king, but was unsuccessful in convincing him to remain detached from the fray. It seemed that King Abdullah was

---

23 Shades of our earlier hero, Haym Salomon, who provided emergency funding for George Washington's army at Valley Forge in 1779!

now taking a middle ground – neither for nor against attacking Jewish forces – at odds with his prior agreement.

What followed now were days of the Yishuv leadership promulgating their declaration of independence. US Secretary of State George Marshall warned the Yishuv that if they proceeded, the Americans would not rescue them from an Arab invasion of their new country. He even threatened to stop moneys from American Jews from reaching the Yishuv and made other threats to the UN regarding partition. Golda would not listen. She insisted that they needed to go all the way: "The world is waiting for our announcement. If we don't make it now, we never will." Six of the ten Cabinet members swung to Golda's position, but many issues were still outstanding – Jerusalem, passports, state symbols, and Arab rights, to name a few. The British Mandate was due to expire on May 15, 1948, so a meeting was held in secret (to avoid British intervention) on the matter of declaring statehood. At four o'clock in the afternoon on May 14, at the Tel Aviv Art Museum, under a massive portrait of Theodor Herzl, David Ben-Gurion (in a suit and tie, for once) opened the meeting. "Hatikvah," the new national anthem, was played. David spoke about the birthplace of the Jewish people and their historic right to a Jewish state, and declared the establishment of a Jewish state in Palestine called the State of Israel!

One by one, the signatories walked to the front of the hall to sign the parchment. Each signed with a newly adopted Hebrew name, except our heroine Golda Meir, who signed "Golda Meyerson." She later said, "From my childhood in America, I learned about the Declaration of Independence and the geniuses who signed it. I couldn't imagine these were real people, doing something real. And here I am signing it – actually signing a declaration of independence. I didn't think it was due me, that I, Goldie Meyerson, deserved it, that I had lived to see the day. My hands shook. We had done it. We had brought the Jewish people into existence."

Golda's job was not done; she faced many more challenges following the creation of the State of Israel. She returned to the United States later that year to raise more money (another $50 million) for Israel's defense. In 1949, she was named minister of labor at a time of severe economic hardship. She successfully instituted rationing to shore up the nation during the crisis. Once, after a series of assaults on women, one minister called for barring women from the streets at night, but Golda protested, "It's the men who are attacking the women, not the other way around. If there's to be a curfew, let the men stay at home!"

In 1956, she became Israel's foreign minister, under Prime Minister Ben-Gurion, and was the architect of extending assistance to developing Arab nations of both money and technicians. Reverend Billy Graham once asked her for the secret of their success, and she replied to him, "We go there to teach, not to preach."[24] She worked eighteen-hour days, and finally resigned in 1965 after much illness and many years of exhausting work. But after only a few years in retirement, she became secretary general to Prime Minister Levi Eshkol and was there to support him during the 1967 war.

After Israel won its famous overwhelming victory in that year, our heroine Golda said, "There is nothing Israel wants so much as peace – with all the bleakness of the desert, the desert of hate around us is even more bleak." She wanted peace, but had a reputation for stubbornness: "Hitler took care of six million Jews. If we lose a war, that's the end, forever – and we disappear from the earth."[25] They wanted to remain alive!

Finally, in 1969, the Labor Party selected her as its candidate for prime minister. She said that this was not the retirement she had had in mind: "Being seventy is not a sin. It's not a joy, either." But she accepted and went on to win the election – she was now prime minister of Israel – in spite of an adversary, Moshe Dayan, Israel's legendary war hero, who had coveted the premiership. She was also a lady prime minister who had beaten out two more popular male candidates – Dayan and Yigal Allon.

Golda became a very down-to-earth and yet very decisive leader for Israel. Once, when US Senator Francis Church, of the Senate

---

24 Ann Atkins, *Golda Meir: True Grit* (Ashland, OH: Flash History Press, 2015), 248.
25 Atkins, *Golda Meir*, 189.

Foreign Relations Committee, came to visit, she disappeared into the kitchen of her home. The senator followed her and saw her cooking. Golda asked, "You came to help?" With his affirmative reply, she politely refused, insisting that he return to the living room while she prepared breakfast. "But there are a few things you can help me with," she added. "Phantoms, land-to-air missiles, and help Russian Jews to emigrate!"

The Israeli public grew to love our tough old Golda. Her approval ratings hit 61 percent in April after just one month in office – and 89.9 percent in July 1969. Amazing numbers! She did have difficult moments, however, particularly with the Labor Party, and she paid a price – strikes and a labor collapse. In 1971, then again in 1972, she hung on despite her extreme fatigue, getting President Nixon to deliver military equipment – jet fighters, army weapons, and ammunition. The Israeli economy was also booming, and finally her party colleagues begged her to stay on. She wavered, and then relented, flattered at the enthusiastic support. She would continue in office.

On the twenty-fifth anniversary of Israel's Independence Day, May 14, 1973, Golda turned seventy-five years old. She had been in office for four years and was very popular in Israel, as well as being one of the most admired women in America and Britain. Golda, though, was both tired and sick. She was ready to leave. But she persevered, until at last an event occurred that would tarnish her politically.

On September 25, 1973, Golda was startled at secret news from King Hussein of Jordan: Syria was preparing a war against Israel! She met with Defense Minister Moshe Dayan, who assured her that there was no need to be alarmed – even though the head of Israel's military intelligence in Jordan had warned of war on the horizon. Golda, attending a meeting in Europe, was called by her aide Galila, who said that security on Israel's borders was not looking good. Also, Israeli intelligence had discovered that a division of Egyptian troops was heading toward the Suez Canal, and 120,000 Egyptian reservists had been called up. Dayan scoffed at this, deeming it only a large military exercise. He also dismissed a US intelligence report of the deployment of Egyptian commandos. Dayan and Eli Zeira, the intelligence director, both believed that the Syrians would not wage war without the Egyptians, who had no long-range bombers to deploy.

Compounding this error, it was only five months previously that Eli Zeira had grown alarmed enough about Egyptian troop movements to prepare for a defensive war. Golda mobilized Israel's reserves, costing Israel $35 million – but there was no attack. Israel could not afford to mobilize its army at every threat on its borders; it had a small standing army and relied on a reservist call-up to defend itself. In early October, Golda was assured again at a cabinet meeting that nothing threatening was afoot. She remained troubled – there were conflicting intelligence reports, and now Israeli troops on the border could see enemy activity.

At another meeting with Dayan and Zeira, she expressed her feeling that something was afoot and called an emergency cabinet meeting. The meeting was inconclusive; the ministers indicated that Israel should delay mobilizing its forces. But they did authorize Golda to call up the reserves – if necessary. It was Yom Kippur, the holiest day of the Jewish year, and Israel was still and silent, with two-thirds of the army on vacation or home. Golda too was at home for dinner, and then went to bed, but did not sleep at all. At 3:30 a.m., the telephone rang with a message – Egypt and Syria would attack at sundown.

At 8:00 a.m., Golda was openly fighting Dayan and Dado Elazar, her chief of staff. Dado wanted to launch a preemptive air strike, but Dayan rejected this as a precipitous move. Golda had to make a momentous decision here. What to do? She was told in a phone call from American Secretary of State Henry Kissinger not to issue a preemptive strike. Finally, in the early afternoon, as the Yom Kippur morning services were ending, air-raid sirens shattered the quiet of the holy day. In the south, over a hundred Egyptian jets attacked southern command posts, another two thousand Egyptian guns shelled Israeli positions, and four thousand infantrymen began crossing the Suez Canal. The Israeli soldiers were astonished. They hunkered down, unable to combat this onslaught of new weaponry.

In the Golan Heights, the Syrians were moving assault tanks and armored personnel carriers through the area, supported by surface-to-air missiles – the situation looked bleak there as well.

Golda's advisors now knew they had to act. Moshe Dayan, however, was entirely negative; knowing he had been wrong, he was thinking in a way that was hampering Israel's chances for survival. "We can't stop them," was his comment to the Israeli command in the north. Dayan even offered Golda his resignation, but she refused it. Dado Elazar, calm and collected, had to change the military's outlook, and quickly.

Our heroine was now facing her greatest challenge – the survival of Israel was at stake. Her critics had categorized her as inflexible, overbearing, and ruling with an iron hand. Now these qualities would be tested. Without the support of her defense minister, Dayan, she was now the generalissimo. This old Jewish grandmother was now running the show. She drafted former IDF Chief of General Staff Haim Bar-Lev to assess the north; David "Dado" Elazar recommended withdrawal from the Sinai, to new positions. Golda worried whether Kissinger would supply arms to Israel, as she had complied with his request not to strike preemptively. By the third day, Israel was pushing back the Syrian onslaught and the Egyptian advance had been stopped, with Bar-Lev taking charge there. Golda sought new supplies from the United States, but Kissinger wanted to prevent an Israeli victory that would humiliate the Arabs. He resisted Golda's request for substantial reinforcements, mainly planes, and blocked the request of Israel's Ambassador Simcha Dinitz as well. Kissinger blamed the Defense Department – "the bureaucracy" – for the delays, but he was the one obstructing in that situation; it was a very troubling double-dealing with Israel.

Golda finally had to act. Time was passing, Israel needed to win the battles in both the north and south, and even President Nixon's order for Israeli aid was being delayed. Golda even personally called members of the US Congress for help, impressing upon them that if she *had* preempted a strike, counter to American request, their situation would be different.

At last, President Nixon, seeing that Russia was airlifting massive amounts of supplies to the Arabs, acted; he ordered an immediate military resupply operation to Israel. Secretary Kissinger again attempted to restrict the action, by limiting the number of planes to be used! President Nixon overruled him, and wave after wave of C-5A Galaxy transport planes brought much-needed bombs, missiles, and ammunition to Tel Aviv.

The Israelis, under Golda and General Bar-Lev, commenced offensive operations, and on the Sukkot holiday were pushing the Egyptians back, almost reaching Cairo in the counter-assault! Even in the north, the IDF soldiers were racing to retake their old positions. But Kissinger was at it again: he wooed the Russians into imposing a cease-fire on Israel. Golda was livid with him – again. He had done this without consulting her, the prime minister! He also required a truce, in twenty-four hours. Not thirty-six hours, not forty-eight hours, but twenty-four! Golda felt that Kissinger was trying to snatch victory away from Israel! Finally, she agreed to accept, if Kissinger would come to Israel to finalize the terms of the agreement.

Her first words to Kissinger upon his arrival were "Why didn't you contact us during negotiations?" After hearing his explanation, that the Soviets had jammed the radio on his plane, Golda responded, "Then how did you stay in touch with your president?" Golda insisted on candor from her guest and questioned everything. She suspected that Kissinger was trying to appease the Arabs, hoping to avert the threat of an oil embargo to the United States. The standoff ended when Golda and her cabinet, after an all-night session, agreed to the cease-fire – although Israel had the Egyptian Third Army surrounded.

Kissinger had won, but Golda had also stood strong, reminding her cabinet that maintaining good relations with the United States was more important than capturing Egypt's army. Sometimes a small country like Israel has to give in to the "only real friend" it has in the world.

Israel had suffered 2,700 casualties, a profound blow to the small country. Golda Meir, to her dying day, regretted that she had not followed her instincts and called up the reserves days before the war.

She had listened to military intelligence experts who saw no reason to mobilize – but they had been wrong! Her party suffered because of this national misstep, and on June 4, 1974, Golda resigned as prime minister.

In her final years, she evolved into an elder statesman and beloved public citizen. Her image regained its luster, and her reputation as a philosopher-comedian became legend. As a politician and Jewish nationalist, Golda was consistent, strong in her resolve, and undisturbed by self-doubts. Her cause – the Zionist cause – she considered moral, historical, and politically imperative.

At the end of her life, Golda still felt guilt about her neglect of her children and her husband Morris (in spite of all their separations, they still remained a married couple until his death in 1951). Golda was, as she would later describe, the "type of woman who cannot remain at home; in spite of the place her children and family fill in her life, her nature demands something more. She cannot let her children narrow her horizon. For such a woman there is no rest."[26]

It was discovered when she died in December 1978, at age eighty, that for twelve years she had been suffering from leukemia.

Golda Meir was a titan of modern Zionism, a history-making national leader, and one of the most accomplished women of the twentieth century. Golda was truly a Jewish heroine of the ages. Rest in peace, Golda. You will always be loved and admired.

---

26 Quoted in Israel Shenker, "Golda Meir: Peace and Arab Acceptance Were Goals of Her Five Years as Premier," *New York Times*, December 9, 1978, http://www.nytimes.com/learning/general/onthisday/bday/0503.html.

11. Menachem Begin

||||||||||||||||||||||||||||||||||||||||||||||||||||||||

Afitting conclusion to our examination of a selection of amazing Jewish heroes down through the ages is a man who became one of the most prominent leaders of the Jewish people in the twentieth century. One tenet of that greatness that sustained him throughout his entire life: "From my early youth, I had been taught by my father – who...went to his death at Nazi hands voicing the liturgic declaration of faith in God and singing...'Hatikvah' – that we Jews were to return to *Eretz Israel*. Not to 'go' or 'travel' or 'come' – but to return."[27]

Our hero Menachem Begin was born in 1913 in the Russian-Polish town of Brisk to Ze'ev Dov and Chasia Begin. He received his name because his birth came four days after Tisha b'Av, the Jewish holiday mourning the destruction of the Temples in Jerusalem, and *menachem*, in Hebrew, means "the comforter."

This was on the eve of World War I, chaotic times. The war was tearing lives apart. Menachem did not know his grandparents. What he did learn about was the misery of the ebb and flow of power among the Russians, Germans, and Poles. Like Zionism, Polish nationalism, with its deep resentment of European occupation, was so potent a force that countries like Russia were determined to extinguish Poland completely, to squelch that humanistic spirit!

The Begin family fled the country during the war, and afterward when they returned to Brisk they were very poor, almost destitute. Menachem was six, and he and his family subsisted on the charity of the various local Jewish organizations. They were also very religious,

---

27 This and all other quotations in this chapter are noted in Daniel Gordis, *Menachem Begin: The Battle for Israel's Soul* (New York: Schocken, 2014), unless otherwise indicated.

and so Menachem was sent first to a *cheder* (a small religious school) and then to a local religious Zionist school, where he remained until high school.

Our Menachem's first great influence was his father. Ze'ev Dov Begin had organized a local Jewish self-defense force in 1905 after a wave of anti-Jewish pogroms had swept the city. His father, Menachem would later write, was a "defender of his brethren against attacks, pogroms, and oppression." Ze'ev Begin also encouraged his three children to speak only Hebrew as their native tongue, calling Polish an "anti-semitic language." Thus Jewish pride was instilled in Menachem and informed everything he said and did. The values Ze'ev drilled into his children were respect for others, love for Zion, pride in being a Jew, and faith that in the future a Jewish state would be established.

It should be noted that Menachem's early childhood years in Brisk were not easy. He suffered much antisemitic treatment at the hands of his fellow Polish students. Many times as a youngster he was beaten and bullied for one reason and one reason only – he was a Jew. His father was also very strict and a strong advocate for German culture. But at the same time, family life at the Begin home was warm and welcoming to friends of all ages. Menachem's education was also enhanced at home, where his father, who knew the Bible by heart, could recite a chapter from the Torah by memory after one of his children would begin with a verse.

Our hero was only thirteen years old when his father encouraged him to join Betar, an organization headed by Vladimir Ze'ev Jabotinsky – a man who rejected socialism and advocated the use of force in search of a Jewish homeland. Jabotinsky was a gifted writer and orator who was deeply shaken by the pogroms being perpetrated against European Jews in the early 1900s. Jabotinsky had joined the World Zionist Organization, but became convinced that the current Zionist leadership was too weak and passive for his purposes. This put him at odds with the WZO's long-time president Chaim Weizmann and, later, David Ben-Gurion, who believed that only ongoing cooperation with the British and political negotiation would help them realize their independent Jewish state. Though both the socialists and Jabotinsky's "Revisionist Zionists" believed in the righteousness of a Jewish state, they differed markedly in their approaches. The Revisionists believed that force must be used, if necessary, to achieve their goals, since Jews were being physically threatened in Eretz Israel and elsewhere; militarism was embraced as self-defense. The word *hadar*, broadly defined as "strength and dignity," became a dominant concept for Jabotinsky and, in due course, our hero Menachem Begin.

So it was inevitable that when Menachem first heard Jabotinsky speak, he was overwhelmed. He was consecrated to his ideal forever: "Jabotinsky became God for him," a friend commented. Our hero began wearing the brown Betar uniform everywhere he went and spoke in public weekly. He became a great speaker, and people very quickly took notice. He had a "great talent" in "speaking from the very soul of the shtetl, to make things simple – black and white – and to offer real salvation. Full salvation!"

In the late 1920s while Menachem Begin was rising in the ranks of Betar, the ongoing animosity between Ze'ev Jabotinsky and David Ben-Gurion was escalating. The distrust between them had resulted in acts of violence against Betar members in Palestine, with Revisionists breaking up strikes staged by the Histadrut, the labor organization in Palestine. This festering wound in the Zionist movement was finally checked when Ben-Gurion and Jabotinsky agreed to "refrain from party warfare" at a series of meetings in London in 1934.

In Poland, our hero Menachem had graduated from high school and entered the University of Warsaw in 1931 to study law. While there, he took an official position as Betar's head of organizational efforts and began to speak out publicly for the cause. Also during his studies at the university, he organized Jewish students into a self-defense group to counter antisemitic harassment on campus. He graduated in 1935 but never practiced law.

Menachem was slowly growing up, speaking all around Europe, preaching *hadar*. He came to lead the Organizational Department of Betar and began requiring Betar members to stand at attention for their commanders. (One incident at the Betar World Congress in Krakow, in 1936, saw him sharing the dais with his mentor Jabotinsky.) Menachem was small, frail, and unassuming, with thick glasses, but with his words he could "mak[e] you believe," as one Betar man in the audience remarked.

By 1937, the student began to rival his master and soon was considered by some to be a better orator than his mentor Jabotinsky. Not only was he coming of age as a speaker, but he was now becoming frustrated with Jabotinsky, who was beginning to advocate diplomacy in dealing with the British – just like David Ben-Gurion! Menachem was steeped in the revolutionary Polish nationalism, and so accommodation with the British did not fit his agenda.

Begin's feud with Jabotinsky continued into the late 1930s, as Betar's military organization, the Irgun, was being created in Palestine. Its aim was self-defense, and to that end it stressed the importance of retaliatory counterattacks against the Arabs as a component of self-defense. Menachem further argued that *preemptive* attacks were also necessary. Finally, Begin challenged Jabotinsky at an international Betar conference in Warsaw in 1938, stating that the Zionist movement should conquer the land of Palestine militarily. This drastic suggestion was squelched by Jabotinsky, dismissed as a "creak in a speech that must be suppressed." But in spite of their bitter clashes, Begin was appointed commander of Betar Poland in 1939, in charge of seventy thousand members; he was dedicated to working with the Irgun and its military efforts in Palestine.

Our hero was becoming a strong Zionist leader, but his life also took a different turn at this point. Menachem had met a beautiful, dark-haired girl from Galicia while speaking at a local Betar chapter. The next day he delivered a note to her, saying, "I saw you, my lady, for the first time, but I feel as if I had known you all my life." He then wooed her, and warned her that life with him would be difficult – he was committed to a lifelong battle for a Jewish state – but she was not dissuaded. So Menachem and Aliza were married just one month after their first meeting in Galicia. Jabotinsky attended the ceremony; both men wore Betar uniforms. Menachem had found the love of his life and was not about to lose her by waiting – and he knew deep down she would be his wife – for a lifetime, without a doubt!

Difficult times were in store for Begin. In late 1939, Germany captured the city of Brisk, Poland. The Russians retook it in 1944, but by then the Jewish community of that city had been erased, totally obliterated by the Nazis – almost as if it had not existed for the past five hundred years. This horrific episode resonated with Menachem, because he then knew the need for Jews to protect themselves and to have their own state. Menachem fortunately had boarded one of the last trains out of Warsaw with his bride before the war, hoping to get to Palestine by ship, and so did not witness firsthand the destruction of the city he left behind.

But he had left behind his parents, his brother, and his wife Aliza's sister, not to mention seventy thousand Betar members. Later, he was to find out that his and Aliza's families had been murdered by the Nazis. Why did he leave, saving himself and his wife, but making a decision that would haunt him his entire life? He escaped, along with much of Warsaw's Jewish leadership, first to Vilnius, in Lithuania, and then to eastern Poland, to evade arrest. While in Vilnius, he received a letter from a Betar organizer in Palestine, rebuking him for abandoning his fellow Betar members. Menachem then wanted to return to Poland but was dissuaded by his peers. The rebuke affected his life and his decisions for decades; it hurt him very deeply.

In 1940 another traumatic event took place in Menachem's life: word came from the United States that Menachem's mentor and idol, Jabotinsky, had passed away in Hunter, New York, on a fund-raising trip for Betar. Menachem held a secret memorial service for his friend and father figure – his inspiration, the man who had shaped his lifelong pursuit of Zionism. This service was kept secret because in Vilnius, the government (and likewise the KGB) suspected Betar and Menachem of anti-Soviet propaganda. He was in any event accused of being an "agent of British imperialism," of all things, and was arrested and sentenced to eight years in the Soviet gulag!

While in prison in Russia, our hero was at first treated poorly, forced to sit in a chair for sixty hours against the wall with his knees together. And although he would suffer physical and emotional pain, he would also engage in endless conversations with all who cared to listen – his interrogator, his guards, his translators, and even his cellmates! More than any other topic, he talked about Zionism and refused to deny that he was a Zionist. He repeatedly defended the Jewish right to national self-determination. Once, he butted heads with a fellow prisoner who decried Zionism as anti-Jewish. Begin, a man of rock-solid Jewish faith, argued that Zionism and Judaism were inseparable – neither made sense without the other. He said that "man understands there are things he cannot fathom by rationality and so he believes in a higher power."

Menachem tried to observe Jewish holidays while in prison, refusing his daily soup ration in October 1940, on Yom Kippur, the Day of Atonement, despite his ravaging hunger. His cellmates gladly ate his portion, quickly and with great appreciation.

When Menachem's anti-Zionist friend Garin lay sick and dying, he requested of his fellow prisoners to sing "Hatikvah," the Jewish national anthem. Menachem mused, "When the time comes, after much tribulation, what does 'the father of Pravda' [the Communist Party] remind himself of? *Lashuv* – return. To return to the land of our fathers." Menachem was consoled by this. He knew his dream would someday become a reality; to him this was the proof – when this non-believer recanted on his deathbed and returned to his roots, his religion, his ancient homeland!

While still languishing in prison, Begin found out that officials in the United States were trying to secure his release. But in June 1941, when the Soviet Union and Poland formed an alliance against Germany, all Polish prisoners in Soviet camps were released anyway. In September 1941, our hero joined the Polish army-in-exile as a corporal. After traveling through southern Russia and the Middle East with General Anders, they made their way to Palestine in April 1942. He was twenty-nine years old and still wore his Polish uniform, but – for the first time in his life – he felt he was home, at last!

Anders then gave Menachem a choice: fight the Nazis in Europe, or stay in Palestine to fight for a Jewish state as a Polish soldier! (Polish officers were sympathetic to the Zionist cause.) He chose the latter, and in December 1942 he joined up with the Polish army in Palestine. At the same time, he established himself as a leader with the Irgun and Betar organizations. For one more year he worked for the Polish army, and finally, on January 26, 1944, he was given his final discharge and was thus free to become the commander of the Irgun in Palestine.

He was a surprising choice for this position, since he was a cultural outsider in so many ways: he was Polish, not really a soldier, had a non-Hebraized name (unlike many other senior Irguniks such as Avraham Tehomi, Aryeh Mazali, and Yaakov Tavin, not to mention leading figures of the Yishuv like Ben-Gurion and Levi Eshkol). He was truly an outsider, but he was who he was – a determined militarist. So he began with an announcement in February 1944: "The blood of our people cried out to us from the foreign soil on which it had been shed. Had we anything to lose?" Our hero was referring to the news of the slaughter of Jews in Germany and Poland, the many broken promises of the British, and to the fact that Jews were now going to be aggressive in pursuing their homeland – he declared a revolt against the British. He was called an outlaw terrorist by the British, who placed a bounty of ten thousand pounds on his head! So to avoid arrest, Menachem went underground for four years, assuming different identities, including those of a law student, a Rabbi Sassover, and finally a Dr. Koenigshoffer, constantly altering his appearance, with and without a beard. He refused to be captured by the British "occupiers."

Our hero's goal, as leader of the Irgun movement, was to revolt against and undermine the British presence in Palestine. The British had reasoned that their purpose in assuming the mandate was to protect the Jews of the Yishuv from the Arabs. Menachem's purpose, however, was to show the British and the world that the Jews were capable of defending themselves – period.

At this point, an event occurred that would totally divide the leaders of the Zionist movement, David Ben-Gurion and our hero Menachem Begin. In November 1944, Lechi, the extreme militant breakaway from the Irgun, assassinated Lord Moyne, the British minister of state, in Cairo. A few members of the Lechi group were apprehended for this crime by the British authorities and eventually hanged in March 1945. The British public was outraged by the homicide, and Winston Churchill warned the Yishuv that this gangster violence would seriously jeopardize the British position. The British sought to destroy the Jewish underground, as did many Yishuv leaders, amazingly, who felt British sympathy was necessary for the establishment of a Jewish state. From November through February, the mainstream Yishuv organizations and leaders assisted the British in their search for the underground members; Jews were now turning in their fellow Jews, yet Menachem did not stop the struggle against British rule. Despite being pursued, even hated by Ben-Gurion, Menachem did not condone the Lechi's killing of Lord Moyne; they had acted alone. But Menachem was still going to limit his fight to the British – he had a deep-seated humanism and felt that the Jewish people and Jewish political sovereignty trumped everything else. He consciously avoided a civil war between Jewish factions, and more than once.

This unity soon paid off and played a significant role in the Zionist struggle. In 1945, the Yishuv and its leadership became infuriated with new British restrictions on Jewish immigration, particularly since hundreds of thousands of Holocaust survivors in European displaced persons camps were anxiously waiting for transport to Palestine. In October, the Haganah, Irgun, and Lechi signed an agreement to work together against the British. They were going to coordinate attacks and operations targeting strategic points and symbols of British power. Our hero Menachem's philosophy of military dissent was making a difference.

Soon, many coordinated attacks took place – supplies and bridges were blown up, preventing the movement of goods and men, and the British were furious. On June 29, 1946, the British placed all the major Jewish cities on lockdown, 2,700 men were arrested, including many leaders of the Yishuv, and weapons were confiscated. The day became known as "Black Saturday." More importantly, word also reached the remaining leaders of the Yishuv that the British had secured valuable documents linking the official Yishuv leadership with the revolt – a very troubling bit of information. They assumed these documents had been taken to the King David Hotel, where the British military and intelligence headquarters for Palestine were housed. These documents would allow the British to arrest and possibly execute the most important leaders of the Yishuv, including Golda Meir. Our hero Menachem had to act, and decisively. He received a note from the head of the Haganah, Moshe Sneh, authorizing the bombing of the King David Hotel – Begin's Irgun would carry it out. Haganah's rationale was that since the British had attacked their government body and sought to paralyze it, they were justified in returning the favor.

It should be noted that Menachem always demanded that his commanders do everything possible to avoid civilian deaths. This was his legacy from Ze'ev Jabotinsky, his mentor. The Irgun therefore planned to warn all civilians who worked in the building – Jewish, Arab, and British – to evacuate. A 45-minute warning was suggested, but was vetoed by Sneh, who said that with such a warning the British "could save documents as well as people." Finally, a half-hour's notice was settled upon, with appropriate warnings in Hebrew, Arabic, and English.

Behind the scenes, Chaim Weizmann had called off the operation, threatening Moshe Sneh that such an act would split the Yishuv. Our hero now saw the Haganah as cowards unwilling to fight for a Jewish state, so two days later when Moshe Sneh delayed the strike again, Menachem agreed to one last delay – but no more. Menachem also pledged to coordinate the Irgun's attack with the other underground groups and to abide by the Haganah's leadership. Finally, after another three days, Menachem called for the operation to take place at last on July 22. Sneh asked for another delay, and got no response from Menachem, even though the Haganah had been given veto power over any operation! Menachem would no longer allow delays due to Haganah cowardice – the Irgun would act.

Finally, on July 22, 1946, seven five-hundred-pound bombs rigged inside empty milk containers detonated in the basement of the hotel. The death toll was heavy: ninety-two people died that day – twenty-eight British, forty-seven Arabs, and seventeen Jews, including one Irgun militant. Menachem became distraught and agitated, even when told that the warnings had been given per his orders. The British had refused to evacuate the building. Even so, Begin released a statement afterward, praising the Hebrew soldiers who followed their orders with "strength and sacrifice" and blaming the British "experts" who took it upon themselves to remove the explosive devices, even though the slightest touch…would have caused them to detonate. Therefore, the loss of civilian lives falls on [the British] and only on them." In other words, the British could have avoided the killing of innocents by heeding the Irgun's warnings, and they did not do so! Menachem felt the casualties had not been the Irgun's intention and were not their responsibility.

In British and American newspapers, animosity toward the Zionists and their operation reached a peak. In the Yishuv, Ben-Gurion and the Haganah denied any involvement in the attack, but Menachem assumed full responsibility and never apologized: "A revolution…does not aim at instilling fear. Its object is to overthrow a regime and to set up a new regime in its place…. Tyranny is armed…. Fighters for freedom must arm; otherwise they would be crushed."

In February 1947, seven months later, the British announced their intention to leave Palestine. Nine months later, the United Nations voted to create a Jewish state, and not long after that, the British presence was gone forever from the Holy Land. Had Menachem's acts of violence been justified?

The united Hebrew Resistance movement was dissolved in the aftermath of the King David bombing. Menachem led the Irgun in a series of operations throughout Palestine. One raid against a British headquarters south of Tel Aviv, in March 1946, saw thirty to forty Jewish fighters storm and overwhelm the British. They successfully raided the ammunition depot, but two Irgun soldiers were unfortunately captured by the British. They were sentenced to death by hanging, after refusing clemency and rejecting the British court's legitimacy and authority.

Menachem was furious. After the horror and humiliation of the Holocaust, he was not about to let Jews hang in the name of British justice, the same British who were preventing tens of thousands of displaced European survivors from reaching their homeland's shores. Those British occupiers, who offered Jews no safe harbor, should not also be permitted to hang Jews battling for independence, for freedom! Menachem vowed that he would respond. It was a matter of *hadar* – Jewish dignity, Jewish self-respect!

So the official Irgun underground radio station issued a warning to the British: if the captured fighters would be hanged, they would answer "gallows with gallows." Menachem was telling the British that the Jews of the Yishuv were victims no more, that they would retaliate for any actions against their fighters. This was followed by an Irgun kidnapping of five British officers. The British relented, and after secret negotiations the captured soldiers' sentence was commuted to life imprisonment.

Begin was pleased with this decision – he had for the first time seen the British reverse a final verdict of hanging. Other events also suggested that the Jewish image was changing. For instance, the British practice of flogging Jewish prisoners was halted. Power was reaping rewards; Menachem had won a second round. Soon, British soldiers were being restricted in their movements in Palestine, and non-essential Britons were being asked to leave the country. The British were reeling from Menachem's actions, but would they continue their positive actions?

On April 14, 1947, the British secretary transferred four captured Irgun fighters to a heavily guarded prison in Acre, in the north. The Irgun had believed that there was a postponement in effect, so they continued to hold captive the British officer and judge whom they had kidnapped. Two days later, on April 16, the four Irgun fighters were hanged without any notice to the Irgun at all – without clergy present, in a violation of British protocol. The four went to their deaths singing "Hatikvah."

Soon after, at the end of July 1947, a ship called the *Exodus* was set to arrive in Haifa with 4,500 Jewish immigrants on board, in defiance of the British White Paper restricting immigration. The British seized this ship of homeless refugees, survivors of the ravages of the Nazi war machine, and sent it back to Germany, of all places! Pressure on Britain increased. The world was repulsed by this gruesome act, but as Winston Churchill had said, "If you're in it to win, you fight to win," an attitude that Menachem actually agreed with.

What did the British do next? In a raid gone bad at Acre Prison, they captured three more Irgun fighters. They too were tried and sentenced to hang. Menachem tried this time to resolve the situation through the United Nations – peacefully, bloodlessly – an attempt at a very humanistic resolution. This was doomed, however, and on July 29, 1947, Yaakov Weiss, Avshalom Haviv, and Meir Nakkar were hanged by the British in Acre Prison.

Menachem had anticipated this possible scenario and had two British sergeants captured from the coastal town of Netanya. Calls for their release echoed throughout the Yishuv – condemning any acts of reprisal as "bloodthirsty" and "unforgivable." Menachem faced a very difficult dilemma, "the most difficult decision of my life," he would later say. On the evening of his thirty-fourth birthday, Menachem gave the order and the two British soldiers were hanged. A note was left near one: "[This was a] sentence [for] the criminals who belong to the criminal Nazi British army of occupation."

The British were humiliated – again. Riots broke out in both Britain and Palestine; demoralized British police in Palestine even went on a rampage, firing on civilian buses, destroying property, killing civilians. In Britain, Jewish businesses were attacked, Jewish centers vandalized, and synagogues burned down. Things were going very badly and getting out of hand for the Yishuv. Menachem would admit later that the hanging of the British soldiers was a brutal act, but that after this episode there were no more hangings in Palestine.

In our stories of Jewish heroes, like David Ben-Gurion and Golda Meir, we often speak of the military struggle beginning with Israel becoming a state, on May 14, 1948. But in the months leading up to that declaration, Arab armies had massed on Israel's borders, and the roads leading to Jerusalem were blocked by Arab bands. The Haganah had to clear these roads if food, fuel, and reinforcements were to reach Jerusalem. They also needed to capture a key Arab village – Deir Yassin – which was strategically located for the impending battle over Jerusalem. The western entrances to Jerusalem were threatened by potential Arab hostilities, so the Haganah partnered with the Irgun to subdue the small Arab town. On April 9, 1948, equipped with a sound truck warning of the impending attack, Irgun militants, along with Lechi forces, moved into Deir Yassin, where they encountered sniper fire and fierce Arab resistance. A dozen Arab homes were blown up, and many residents were killed. The number of men, women, and children killed was disputed by both sides, ranging from about a hundred to 250.

Rumors and disinformation reached beyond Israel to the international community. Menachem would unfortunately be blamed for the "Deir Yassin massacre," which infuriated David Ben-Gurion and reignited the feud between the two. Menachem would again take personal responsibility for the attack, and the Irgun expressed "great sorrow for the wounded women and children." But now Begin also blamed the Haganah for giving the green light to the Irgun for the operation and then holding them responsible for it. Menachem was nevertheless ultimately blamed by the Ben-Gurion government anyway; they tried to disavow these acts of force. The final analysis showed that Menachem Begin had not overreached: he did not shoot residents in cold blood or commit other heinous acts, including rape. But the action at Deir Yassin had the desired effect on the many village Arabs in the territory – a mass exodus began to take place, with many thousands of Arab residents leaving their towns. Now, finally the Jerusalem road had been opened, and soon thereafter, with the British soldiers leaving, our hero would come out of hiding for the first time in four years!

Menachem Begin, the underground commander, was not invited when Israel declared its independence on May 14, 1948, but the next night, in a radio speech, he said, "This event has occurred after seventy generations of dispersion and unending wandering of an unarmed people, and after a period of almost total destruction of the Jew as Jew. Thus, although our suffering is not yet over, it is our right and our obligation to proffer thanks to the Rock of Israel and his Redeemer for all the miracles that have been done this day, as in those times. We therefore can say with full heart and soul on this first day of our liberation from the British occupier: Blessed is he who has sustained us and enabled us to have reached this time." (In Hebrew, "*she'hecheyanu v'kiyemanu v'higiyanu la'zman hazeh.*")

This speech reflected Menachem's deep belief in the Almighty God; it was notable because Ben-Gurion's Declaration speech did not explicitly mention God at all. The ongoing bitterness between the two great leaders would soon erupt again, and again, repeatedly threatening the newly established state.

Even with Israel reborn as an independent state, animosity continued among the several paramilitary factions as they eventually solidified into the new IDF. Our hero Menachem had been the leader of the Irgun; now he was asked by Ben-Gurion to step down and mainstream his fighters into the Israel Defense Forces, which was run exclusively by the former Haganah – the same Haganah that had previously persecuted Irgun members. Begin insisted it would be difficult to serve under superiors whom Irgun members had been trained to hate. Both sides were ill at ease with the prospect of uniting, but finally, two weeks after independence, Begin announced an unofficial agreement that the IDF would absorb the Irgun, which would no longer operate independently in Israel.

But what about its operations abroad? The Paris Irgun office declared that Jerusalem – which was not part of the agreement, was still in danger – and needed to be defended. By whom? The Irgun, of course. So, with an arms embargo by the UN still in place (to maintain a cease-fire between the Israelis and Arabs), an American Irgun operative named Hillel Kook purchased a US Navy landing ship to deliver 940 immigrants, plus weapons and ammunition, to Israel. The ship was called the *Altalena* ("seesaw"), and began its voyage to Israel without our hero Menachem's knowledge. Secrecy would be all-important to the success of the illegal adventure – no cable or radio transmissions to the leadership in Paris – as Menachem was expressly committed to the cease-fire in place.

It should be noted that this merger between the Irgun and the IDF was ambiguous in many respects. The inclusion of Jerusalem in the agreement, at that time not a part of Israel, was not clear. Ben-Gurion had given up on retaking the city, while our hero Menachem still had fighters stationed there. And since the Irgun branches abroad continued to function, they saw their role as liberators of Jerusalem, in spite of the vaguely worded military union agreement. In addition, Irgun members viewed the arms embargo against Israel as grossly unfair. Why? Because the British and other supporters could still ship arms and ammunition to Arab countries like Jordan and Egypt – where they could then fall into the hands of the Palestinian Arabs. A bad scenario for Israel.

When Menachem learned of the approaching *Altalena* via BBC radio, he sent a cable to the ship with instructions to stay away. This cable, for whatever "technical reasons," never reached the *Altalena*. Finally, Menachem went to the government and informed Ben-Gurion that he had not authorized the ship to come to Israel.

A critical series of events now took place. First, if the ship was allowed to land in Israel, who would control the arms on board? Second, who would use the weapons – the Irgun in Jerusalem, or the IDF? Remember that Menachem Begin and David Ben-Gurion greatly distrusted each other – the King David Hotel bombing and the Deir Yassin massacre were both incidents Ben-Gurion blamed on our hero! The Haganah leader, Yisrael Galili, agreed to give the Irgun 20 percent of the weapons, but Ben-Gurion, at an emergency meeting of the cabinet, accused Menachem of concealing the *Altalena*'s passage until it was already at sea – a false presentation of the actual facts. Ben-Gurion was afraid that the Irgun was going to challenge the IDF, and by extension his authority as prime minister of Israel. At that time David Ben-Gurion truly hated our hero and viewed him as disloyal to the fledgling state.

The *Altalena* landed north of Tel Aviv, at Kfar Vitkin, to avoid the UN observers. Slowly, the unloading began. After the Holocaust survivors were allowed to disembark, the Haganah showed up in full force. They announced that the ship and its cargo were under the control of the Israeli government, but Begin was not about to give in to this ultimatum, not believing the army had "bad intentions." The Irgun continued unloading the weapons.

For some unknown reason, a shot rang out from the IDF – or was it the Irgun, firing a warning shot? Either way, our hero instructed his fighters "not to fire back." But soon, regardless, Jews were killing Jews. Menachem quickly boarded the ship and ordered it to set sail for Tel Aviv while the fighting continued on the beach. When the *Altalena* reached Tel Aviv it ran aground, in full view of the city. When Menachem finally began unloading weapons from the ship, he indicated that they were "for ourselves and for you [the Haganah]. We have come to fight together. We shall not fire; we shall not fight our brothers." His plea was not heeded, however, and a full-scale firefight ensued, with Irgun fighters ignoring Menachem's orders.

Ben-Gurion was determined to use force to subdue the *Altalena*. After an interim cease-fire in the afternoon, called so that the wounded could be moved to safety, the fighting resumed. Our hero was convinced he was being targeted by Ben-Gurion, in addition to Ben-Gurion's attempts to sink the ship. Finally, the IDF brought cannons to the beach to shell the *Altalena*. After three misses, a fourth shot hit the ship, causing fire and billowing smoke. Menachem was forced by his men to go ashore, after someone else raised the white flag of surrender. He did not want to leave his men (the Warsaw incident, where he had left his Betar members, still haunted him), but after the wounded were evacuated, he was put on a launch – he couldn't swim – or did he jump into the water? Either way, the Haganah continued to fire while the Irgun fighters made their way to the beach. Our hero survived, but the toll was horrific: sixteen Irgun members dead, three IDF soldiers dead, and dozens of wounded Jews on both sides.

When Begin finally made it to shore, he went immediately to his house, soaking wet, and without his glasses, which he had lost in the ocean. But now he was totally lost – all his life, he had fled from tragedy and fought for his survival. He had left Brisk in World War II, the Nazis had killed his parents, the Soviets had locked him up, the British had hunted him for four years…and now the Jews, his own brethren, had tried to kill him! Menachem now understood Ben-Gurion's animosity toward him completely.

But in spite of this setback, in spite of Prime Minister Ben-Gurion abrogating their agreements, he gave a speech on the radio. "Do not raise a hand against a brother – not even today…. It is forbidden that a Hebrew weapon be used against Hebrew fighters…. Long live the heroes of Israel!" Begin encouraged his Irgun followers to not seek revenge. "Our enemy is the Arabs, not the Jews," he repeated, over and over!

It should be noted that the *Altalena* incident was a scenario brought about because two of our heroes, Ben-Gurion and Begin, could not or would not make reasonable judgments. Ben-Gurion hated and distrusted Menachem, and feared a potential civil war or coup, which could have placed the new state in jeopardy. Menachem Begin, on the other hand, defended his actions – landing on a high-profile beach, at Tel Aviv, with no escape route – and his assertion that the Haganah too had broken the UN cease-fire when it illegally unloaded arms at Bat Yam the same day as the *Altalena* incident. He also constantly reminded his countrymen that he would not fire on fellow Jews.[28] The various

28 History records that Menachem Begin really was responsible for preventing a civil war, rather than encouraging one. David Ben-Gurion finally admitted, in 1965, after a government inquiry into the *Altalena* incident, "Perhaps I was mistaken." Quoted in Jerold S. Auerbach, *Brothers at War:*

functions of the military were finally united on November 7, 1948; the IDF was now Israel's sole army.

In 1949, Menachem emerged from his absence on the political scene to found a new party – the Herut ("freedom") Party. In the first election, this new party won only fourteen of the 120 seats of Israel's new parliament, the Knesset. The Israeli economy was faltering – 500,000 Holocaust survivors and 700,000 Jews from Arab countries were flooding into the country, straining Israel's minimal resources. In 1951, the Herut party won just eight seats, receiving only 6 percent of the vote. Menachem was dejected and resigned from the party he had created. He was through with politics, or so he thought.

A new chapter would soon change Menachem's political life, however. In March 1951, Ben-Gurion claimed that to compensate Israel for absorbing 500,000 European immigrants, the Allied powers should expend $1.5 billion for "resettlement of the Jewish immigrants...formerly under Nazi control." This request was made when Israel did not have normal diplomatic relations with Germany – German passports were not recognized in Israel. So despite the fact that the request was made of the Allied powers, Germany's Chancellor Adenauer responded, amazingly, seeking a solution to the refugee issue. But in Israel, the response was furious, with *Ma'ariv*, a leading newspaper, publishing a gruesome editorial cartoon depicting a blood-soaked bag of money being given to an Israeli standing on a bridge over a mass grave, next to a crematorium. The Herut Party was energized by this opportunity for political redemption, and when the editor of *Herut* newspaper visited our hero and challenged him to rise to the occasion as a "moral obligation to your family, your murdered mother," Menachem relented.

Back in the political arena, Menachem delivered a series of speeches focused on the victims, whom he said were being "sold." Ben-Gurion responded by touting the advantages of a flourishing Jewish Israel. At this point, our hero was really back in the fray; his issue was the dignity of the entire Jewish people. His speeches would passionately plead that

Israel and the Tragedy of the Altalena (New Orleans: Quid Pro Books, 2011).

"The most shameful act and event that has ever occurred in the history of our people is about to take place…. We will recall our hallowed fathers, our slaughtered mothers, and our babies who were led by the millions to the slaughter at the hands of the Satan who emerged from the very bottom of hell to annihilate the remnant of our people."

Bitter words were spoken against the agreement with Germany, but Ben-Gurion was not dissuaded from his mission. He considered Menachem a demagogue who invoked God's name, a product of a traditional father and religious schools. For Menachem, the past struggles of the Jewish people in Europe shaped the future; the past would remind Jews of the continuing need for a Jewish state, and our hero Menachem would never abide the negation of all the accomplishments of the Jews of Europe and the Diaspora. Ben-Gurion did not feel the same way – he derided the European Jew as weak-kneed and cowardly, having no soul. Menachem, though, also sought the dignity and respect for the Jewish people in their own state. So the two heroes, though committed to a Jewish future, differed on how to get there.

When the vote by the Knesset was tallied, approving the reparations dialogue, our hero dropped his resistance. But in spite of losing his fight for the dignity and respect of the Jewish people over the reparations from Germany, our hero had emerged as the leader of the Jewish soul. His reputation, tarnished unjustly by the *Altalena* incident, was restored. He was reborn as a true leader; his appeal to Jewish memory of the Holocaust and Jewish survival resonated deeply.

Beginning in 1964, a series of events transpired that would finally define our hero's place in Israel's history books. After Ben-Gurion resigned as prime minister in June 1963, Levi Eshkol succeeded him. Menachem, though a Knesset member, had languished as leader of the opposition party for many years, failing to gain electoral momentum. Israel had also survived a second major war, in 1956, capturing the Sinai Peninsula and Gaza Strip from Egypt. Even Ben-Gurion had come to realize, as Jabotinsky had originally said, that force is sometimes necessary for survival. He was slowly coming around to Menachem's strong belief in *hadar* – Jewish dignity.

But now Ben-Gurion had departed the political arena, and our hero was inching closer to power with his nemesis no longer in the way, no longer blocking him, no longer denouncing him.

One of the first things Menachem did was to work with the new prime minister, Eshkol, to rebury Ze'ev Jabotinsky in Israel. Remember that Menachem had not been able to provide proper burials for his parents or his fellow prisoners from the Soviet and Polish labor camps. He now attended to the final resting place of his inspiration, his mentor, his father figure – Ze'ev Jabotinsky. After Jabotinsky's body was exhumed in New York, along with his wife's, they were flown to Tel Aviv where they were met by three hundred Herut supporters. Former Irgun members placed a sword on Jabotinsky's coffin, after a stop in Ramat Gan, where the caskets were placed beside the monument to Dov Gruner, an Irgun fighter hanged by the British. They were then taken to Mt. Herzl Cemetery in Jerusalem, the national cemetery for fallen Israeli leaders and heroes. At the Knesset the following day, Jabotinsky's accomplishments were extolled – he was now viewed as one of the great leaders of Zionism and one of the founders of Israel. Our hero Menachem's stock was also rising, with Mapai, Ben-Gurion's former party, slowly fading from the scene.

The Six-Day War, in 1967, saw Prime Minister Levi Eshkol call for a national unity government and include our hero Menachem as a cabinet member. The perennial outsider, the opposition leader for so long, was now, finally, part of the government.

It was at this point that Menachem, in an attempt at greater national unity, began floating the idea of bringing David Ben-Gurion out of retirement to serve as prime minister! This was a difficult time for Israel, and Menachem saw Eshkol's leadership as weak. Ben-Gurion declined, however, and said, "If I knew Begin like I know him now, the face of history would have been different." Amazing words from the former adversary who had despised Menachem.

In 1967, Israel did not wait for an impending Egyptian or Arab attack. The Israeli Air Force, in a preemptive strike, decimated the Egyptian Air Force on its home ground. Within a week, Israel controlled the Golan Heights, Jerusalem, and the Sinai Peninsula, tripling the size of the country. Even before the war had faded, our hero was contemplating victory and viewing the unfolding events not just militarily, but through the eyes of Jewish history. He impressed upon the national unity government the importance of each minister and the two accompanying chief rabbis reciting the *she'hecheyanu* and Psalm 126 ("When the Lord brought back those that returned to Zion") on their first official visit to the Western Wall. Our hero was emphatic in viewing this battle in the context of an epic war for the survival of the Jewish people – since time immemorial.

Over the next few years, our Menachem continued to oppose the Alignment Party, the Labor alliance of the Mapai, Ahdut HaAvoda, and Mapam Parties. Golda Meir was now prime minister and had a good working relationship with Menachem, who was also close to Ariel Sharon, a founder of a new party called Likud – the Unity Party.

In October 1973, however, Israel's very existence hung in the balance. On the holiest day of the Jewish calendar, Yom Kippur, October 6, the Egyptians and Syrians were poised for an attack. The American secretary of state, Henry Kissinger (a Jewish-born American), refused to provide decisive aid and support for Israel. Ariel Sharon, another great Israeli hero, would save the day for Israel, however, sending troops across the Suez Canal to encircle the Egyptian troops, turning the tide of battle for Israel. Israel went on to win the war, but with a high death toll that left the public demanding answers. An investigative committee uncovered that the high-ranking military officers in the government had ignored significant intelligence reports regarding the imminent attack. Golda Meir was forced to resign as prime minister, with party member Yitzhak Rabin succeeding her.

The Israeli public was growing increasingly disenchanted with Meir and Rabin's Alignment Party. The misconduct of the Yom Kippur War was greatly resented by the Israeli citizenry. The left wing was now perceived as European, white, educated, elite, and out of touch with the lower class. Jewish immigrants from North Africa, Yemen, Iraq, and other countries were also clamoring for change. Menachem, on the other hand, was not seen as an elitist, but as the unified Jewish people's populist, concerned about the Jews of Middle Eastern backgrounds who were overshadowed by the Ashkenazi ruling class.

So in early 1977, an election year in Israel, our hero Menachem was an internationally known figure, but also the source of much division. In America, the Anti-Defamation League derided him, canceling a speaking engagement in Milwaukee because he was not a "mainstream Jewish leader." He was still viewed as a terrorist in Great Britain (recall the King David Hotel bombing and the hanging of British soldiers), and demonstrations there clouded his three-day visit in early 1972. Many in Israel also doubted his potential to become a true leader, a prime minister: he had failed eight times to win election as the leader of the opposition to the Labor Party.

Finally, on May 17, 1977, just after he suffered a debilitating heart attack, Menachem Begin and his party won the majority of seats in the Knesset. Popularly known as the *mahapach* (the upheaval), this victory saw a party other than the Alignment/Mapai win for the first time in Israeli history. This also signaled a fundamental change in Israeli society, where a coalition of socially conservative minorities (Jews from North Africa, the Middle East, and the urban poor) now prevailed. Although our Menachem had been demonized by Labor as totalitarian and extremist, his self-portrayal as a humble and pious leader struck a chord with many who felt abandoned by the ruling party and its ideology. Our hero had lived twenty-nine years before coming to the Holy Land, and he had spent twenty-nine years in the position of opposing the Labor government – but he was now prime minister of the country he had helped to create.

Many Israelis danced in the streets, celebrating this great victory, and our hero quoted from the Gettysburg Address and the Torah when he addressed his new constituents. He also donned a yarmulke and recited the *she'hecheyanu*. No Israeli leader had ever done this before, not even Ben-Gurion when he had declared Israel's statehood.

Menachem would also reiterate who he was. In his first speech as prime minister he said, "The Jewish people has a historic right to the Land of Israel. It is our ancestral homeland and that right is inalienable."[29] Although he was now prime minister, he was and would be unlike any prime minister Israel had elected before. He was Israeli, but first and foremost he was a Jew. When asked, after his victory, how he would lead his government, he responded, "In the style of a good Jew."[30]

In June 1977, an incident occurred that demonstrated our hero's compassion for all humanity, not just Jews. Several dozen Vietnamese refugees had fled North Vietnam in a leaky fishing boat, seeking freedom. With little food and water, they drifted helplessly on the South China Sea for many days. Five ships sailed past them without offering aid. Finally, an Israeli vessel picked them up and brought them on board to safety. After three countries – Japan, Hong Kong, and Taiwan – declined to take them in, even refusing them medical treatment, our new prime minister granted them asylum in Israel. He assured them of good hospitality and promised to help resettle them with jobs and to teach them Hebrew as well! Later, in July, when Menachem was meeting with President Jimmy Carter, he was thanked in a speech that praised his act as "typifying the historic struggle of the people of Israel."

In the summer of 1977, another event helped to further define our hero and his mission as prime minister of Israel. One quality Menachem had acquired from his mentor Jabotinsky was *hadar*, or dignity – which applied not just to Jews but to the dignity of the human condition. Just as Jabotinsky had been opposed to racism in the United States, Begin was opposed to the racism he saw all over the world. In particular, Jews had lived for thousands of years in Ethiopia; these *"falashahs,"* or exiles, were viewed by Menachem as Jews who should certainly qualify for the 1950 Law of Return in Israel.[31]

---

29 Thomas Mitchell, *Likud Leaders: The Lives and Careers of Menachem Begin, Yitzhak Shamir, Benjamin Netanyahu and Ariel Sharon* (Jefferson, NC: McFarland and Co., 2015), 61.

30 Ibid.

31 The Law of Return guaranteed every Jew the automatic right to immigrate to Israel. This law was a response to the boats loaded with Jewish refugees

So, following a rabbinical determination that these Ethiopians were in fact Jewish, many began emigrating to Israel. Over the next ten years, thousands would reach the Holy Land. In May 1979, our hero said, "We will not rest, we shall not be silent, until all the Jews both in Syria and Ethiopia are with us on our land." He expanded Israel's outreach to Syrian Jews as well, although the fruits of that relationship would not be realized until later. But when other Israeli prime ministers extended the rescue of the Ethiopian Jewish people through Operations Moses and Solomon from 1985 through 1991, over twenty-one thousand in all made their aliyah to Israel.

Next our hero Menachem initiated new government programs with the intent of rehabilitating poor neighborhoods in Israel. The goal was to eliminate slum conditions and improve the quality of life; this renewal project had affected over 500,000 people in eighty-two towns by 1983. Menachem also instituted economic policies that enabled Israel to be more competitive in the world marketplace. Menachem's government was driven by his desire to move Israel toward a capitalist economy, in order to yield higher living standards and create a trend toward greater accumulation of consumer goods by the average Israeli.

This approach was diametrically opposed to the Labor government's pursuits, which valued social and government power in bringing about equality. Menachem was a fiscal conservative; the labor governments preceding his were leftist and liberal. These differences, beyond their methods of governing, were also starkly apparent in the differences in their policies regarding the military, religion, labor unions, and socialism.

---

whom no country would take and who were turned back to Europe in the days before World War II (such as in the well-known story of the *St. Louis*). Menachem knew antisemitism, knew what it was to be without a country, knew what life as an exile was like. His worldview encompassed a biblically inspired care for his brethren. When our hero Menachem died in 1997, the Ethiopian Jewish community mourned him deeply. An Israeli Ethiopian ambassador would say: "It was Begin who broke down the walls. He believed that the place of the Ethiopian Jews is in Israel. He saw it as his destiny to bring the community here.... For him it was clear that all Jews should be in Israel. Begin was a warm Jew who loved the Jewish people."

Soon, another stage in Menachem's ascent to greatness began to emerge. Four years after the Yom Kippur War, Prime Minister Begin had clearly expressed, in the course of his relations with other countries like Romania and Morocco, that he was seeking to negotiate with Egypt for peace. President Sadat of Egypt, who had tried and failed to wipe out Israel in 1973, knew that he must now do things differently. So his response to our hero's initiative was, "Can an extremist like Begin really want peace?" (Even Sadat had great respect for Begin's track record for Israeli independence.) When Sadat was assured by President Ceausescu of Romania that Begin was genuinely interested in peace, he was told, "Begin is a hard man to negotiate with, but you can trust him."

So in an address to the Egyptian Parliament in November 1977, Sadat declared, "Israel will be stunned to hear me tell you that I am ready to go to the ends of the earth and even to Israel, to argue with them, in order to prevent one Egyptian soldier from being wounded." What did our Menachem then do? In a radio broadcast that same month, he said he was inviting Sadat to Jerusalem and that he hoped Israel and Egypt could be "real friends and allies." He then reminded Sadat that according to the Koran, Israel's claim to the Holy Land was reiterated by none other than Moses when he said, "O my People, enter the Holy Land which Allah hath written down as yours" (5:21). Menachem wanted to make sure Sadat knew that Begin's Israel was not negotiable – no way!

An official invitation was sent by Menachem Begin to President Sadat in November 1977, an invitation to visit Israel. It was accepted immediately; he would come for peace. It was decided that President Sadat would arrive after sundown, at eight o'clock on a Saturday evening. This was our hero's way of showing the world that his Jewish state, Israel, honored the Sabbath day of rest.

When Sadat arrived at Ben-Gurion Airport, which was festooned with light and color, Prime Minister Begin was there to meet him, accompanied by a military band, as the Egyptian president made his way off the airplane. Sadat was very gracious in greeting Israel's leaders, including Moshe Dayan, Yitzhak Rabin, and even our heroine Golda Meir. He delivered his momentous address to the Knesset and detailed his requirements for peace. Menachem followed, reiterating Israel's claim and historical connection to the Land of Israel. He finished by invoking the psalm where the prophet Zechariah says, "Love, truth, and peace" (Zechariah 8:19).

The negotiations began. Sadat envisioned many things, but did not desire a detailed agreement with specific written language. Menachem, on the other hand, was detail-oriented and wanted things clearly spelled out. The negotiations therefore became very strained, and the American facilitators, like Secretary of State Cyrus Vance, became frustrated with Menachem's intransigence on various issues. Giving the Sinai back to Egypt was not going to hold up the peace talks for our hero, but giving up settlements in the West Bank and Gaza Strip was not acceptable. Our hero's mindset was that the Jewish people had a right to their ancestral homeland – period. In addition, when President Carter entered the fray, he sided with President Sadat, at the expense of Prime Minister Begin. He appeared to view our hero as wanting land, not peace.

Finally, after a meeting in February 1978, President Carter, with President Sadat, declared Israel's settlements in the Sinai illegal, and promised Egypt new military jets! What?! It certainly appeared that the American president was being hostile to Israel! With Begin depressed and physically unwell, the peace talks were moved to Camp David, in Maryland.

Menachem was again pressured by Carter into creating a unique opportunity to either bring peace about or kill the process – "an opportunity which may never come again in our lifetime," said Carter. Menachem, whose view of life was deeply rooted in a historic Jewish consciousness, was not moved. "Our people lived thousands of years before Camp David, and will live thousands of years after Camp David!"[32] The challenge was there – his mentor Ze'ev Jabotinsky had

---

32 Ned Temko, *To Win or to Die: A Personal Portrait of Menachem Begin* (New York: William Morrow, 1987), 223.

said that to achieve an agreement in the present, one must abandon all past attempts to achieve it. In other words, you must start anew! Their peace agreement must be a new beginning.

At Camp David, our hero was under pressure to dismantle the Jewish settlements in the Sinai Peninsula. Menachem was pained by this and saw that these actions could possibly establish a precedent for removing settlers from the West Bank and Gaza too. Finally, Ariel Sharon, who was now minister of defense, convinced Begin to agree on the issue of the Sinai settlements, but not the West Bank. President Sadat would get back the Sinai Peninsula, the issue of Jerusalem's sovereignty was dropped, and any progress on a Palestinian state was avoided in the final agreement. The peace treaty was signed on September 17, 1979, in Washington, DC. This was an agreement of historic proportions, a watershed moment in Middle East history. It was the first time an Arab state recognized Israel's legitimacy, and it continues to serve as a blueprint for resolving the Arab-Israeli conflict. In addition, given Egypt's prominent position in the Arab world and its status as Israel's most powerful enemy, the treaty had far-reaching strategic and political implications.

Menachem's public image as an irresponsible radical was now transformed to that of a statesman of historic stature. When the Nobel Peace Prize was awarded to him, along with President Sadat, in 1978, his lustrous image was further polished and amplified. At the award ceremony, Menachem spoke from the heart, saying, "I have come from the Land of Israel, the land of Zion and Jerusalem, and here I stand in humility and with pride as a son of the Jewish people as one of the generation of the Holocaust and Redemption." He continued with other amazing words, quoting Thomas Jefferson regarding liberty and invoking his mentor Jabotinsky's beliefs by saying, "Fighters for freedom hate war." The story of Israel was not war or peace, but rather peace through strength.

At the closing of this epic ceremony, Menachem felt into his pocket and took out a black silk yarmulke. He placed it on his head, and recited the original Hebrew of the entire Psalm 126 from memory: "A song of ascents; when the Lord brought back those that returned to Zion, we were like unto them that dream" – this was his amazing tribute to a hard-won peace with Egypt.

So our hero had taken a great step forward for peace, and had spoken at the Knesset about the lasting peace they were entering – but in the Middle East, that volatile part of the world, things can change quickly. In 1974, Saddam Hussein, dictatorial leader of Iraq, had started building a nuclear reactor with the technical assistance of the French government. Saddam had gone public with this project, telling a Lebanese publication in 1975 he was constructing a nuclear arms program. He had then threatened to "drown" the Jewish state "with rivers of blood." So this horrific threat from a neighbor was not going to go away. By 1980, Israel had tried and failed to negotiate with France and Italy to cut off their assistance to Iraq, and with the United States to obtain assurances the program would end.

Menachem had been concerned about a nuclear threat to Israel since 1963, calling it the "gravest threat to our future, our security, our existence."

Then, other events occurred that concerned Israel. The Mossad detonated several core reactors in France that were waiting to be sent to Iraq. Also, in June 1980, Egyptian nuclear scientist Yahya El Mashad, who worked for the Iraqis, was found dead – and the Mossad's involvement was suspected. But in 1980, Israel needed to make a hard decision – whether or not to strike and destroy the reactor at Osirak. Would Egypt abrogate the peace agreement if they did so? Would France curtail relations with Israel? Would the United States condemn the attack to protect Arab interests? What was Menachem to do? Shimon Peres, a key political figure in the Alignment Party, was adamant that "this could become a disaster for Israel." Menachem Begin, our hero, contemplated action, but then delayed. Sleepless nights and anxious days followed; Menachem bore an awesome burden, in secret, but it was eating him up. Neither silence nor secrecy was necessary: the United States had been alerted "to do something or we shall have to!"

Menachem was finally convinced that inaction was the more dangerous path to take – soon the reactors would go hot! Prolonging the strike any longer might mean that in a potential future attack, radiation would be released! The decision was finally made. The F-16 pilots were in intensive practice for months – three Israeli pilots even died in training mishaps while preparing for this all-important mission.

Given the go-ahead, the pilots – sons and grandsons of Holocaust survivors – were on their way to the target. They knew that every conceivable type of weaponry would be fired against them when they flew into and out of Baghdad – anti-aircraft guns, ground-to-air missiles, and fighter planes would defend Osirak. But not a single enemy missile or shell touched them. The mission succeeded beautifully – Osirak was destroyed. Israel was safe from a nuclear disaster at the hands of the maniacal Arab dictator Saddam Hussein.

"Only by the grace of God could we have succeeded in that mission," said Menachem.

Operation Opera, as it was called, although successful, was condemned by many foreign governments, including that of the United States. The UN unanimously passed Resolution 487 condemning the attack. But the Begin doctrine had won the day – "On no account shall we permit an enemy to develop weapons of mass destruction against Israel." Our hero won re-election three weeks later. In August 1981, former President Richard Nixon, at a meeting with President Sadat, called Menachem's act irresponsible. Sadat hesitated and then responded, "Yes, he is crazy…probably crazy like a fox." A former enemy, now a strong ally, recognized Menachem's brilliance and resolve.

One final incident attributed to our hero would now resonate with controversy in Israel. The former terrorist had become a devotee of peace, and had won a Nobel Peace Prize. At the same time, the destruction of the Osirak nuclear reactor had demonstrated his talent as a military manager. Even though he was not 100 percent physically fit (he had suffered heart attacks and other ailments), he was leading Israel with resolve and tenacity. But now a new threat to Israel was emerging.

In 1970, a Palestinian leader named Yasser Arafat had attempted to undermine King Hussein and Jordan by launching terror attacks within Jordan itself. This perceived threat to the king's authority necessitated action against the Palestinian Liberation Organization, which Arafat led. Thus, in September 1970, Jordan's army killed thousands of PLO terrorists and expelled the organization from the country – in essence this was Arabs killing fellow Arabs!

Arafat moved his organization to Lebanon and began regularly launching Russian Katyusha rocket attacks against towns in northern Israel. The final straw was the attack on Israel's Coastal Road, where eleven PLO terrorists hijacked a bus on its way to Tel Aviv, killing thirty-eight Israeli civilians and injuring seventy-one others. *Time* magazine called the attack the worst in Israel's history. So Menachem ordered Operation Litani, sending IDF troops to pursue the PLO back toward Beirut. They managed to clear the PLO from southern Lebanon, but many operatives survived and Menachem was still concerned.

The PLO attacks soon began anew. By 1982, more than fifteen thousand Palestinian guerrillas were operating in southern Lebanon, threatening Israel. What would Menachem do? The newly elected American president Ronald Reagan called for restraint. In response, Menachem wrote back, "The purpose of the enemy is to kill Jews. Is there a nation in the world that would tolerate such a situation?" Menachem was bound by his belief that the Jewish state would "never again" allow a foreign enemy to determine their fate. Finally, Menachem promised President Reagan that if Israel did enter Lebanon to pursue the PLO, it would be a limited invasion.

Then, on June 3, 1982, there was an attempt to assassinate the Israeli ambassador in London. Menachem instructed General Ariel Sharon, his trusted defense minister, to initiate "Operation Peace for Galilee," a plan designed to create a forty-mile buffer zone in southern Lebanon to prevent the PLO from shelling Israel. Prime Minister Begin was hoping for a short, limited Israeli involvement that would destroy the PLO's political and military capabilities in southern Lebanon.

This would also change the balance of power in Lebanon to favor the Christian militias, which were friendly with Israel.

Controversial events then unfolded in Lebanon, unforeseen by our hero Menachem. General Sharon's incursion into southern Lebanon rapidly escalated into a larger military operation. The PLO had a well-trained and organized army; they were not the terrorist bands the Israelis had previously encountered. History records conflicting information regarding the actions taken in Lebanon by the Israelis. Many believed that Ariel Sharon would tell Menachem only what he wanted him to hear about the campaign. The proposed limited war, with limited objectives (the forty-mile perimeter), now escalated into a full-scale invasion all the way to Beirut. Others surmised that Ariel Sharon outfoxed Menachem, who was drawn into a battle far more dangerous and complex than the original plan of attack.

Menachem was not well; his heart problems and diabetes had diminished his physical health. He seemed to become dependent on Sharon for all reports and advice on the war. Israeli tanks were in Beirut and casualties were mounting: 216 Israeli soldiers dead, and a thousand more wounded. So even though our hero told the world the PLO was being heavily armed with Soviet weapons and rockets, Israel's allies – mainly the United States and President Reagan – were very upset with Israel's aggressiveness in Lebanon.

Arafat finally left Lebanon to go to Tunisia with many of his fighters. But the war was not over – a bomb planted by a Syrian PLO operative destroyed Christian Phalangist headquarters in Beirut. The Phalanges lost their leader, Bashir Gemayel, in the bombing, and vowed to exact revenge. Menachem now ordered General Sharon to take up defensive positions in Beirut, but what did Sharon do? He said at a cabinet meeting that he wanted the Phalanges to seek revenge on the PLO "with their own methods."

Menachem Begin would deeply regret the events that transpired, because the IDF under Ariel Sharon allowed Phalangist forces seeking revenge on the Palestinians to enter two Palestinian refugee camps, Sabra and Shatila, in Beirut. The Phalangists, still seething and angry over the deaths of Gemayel, their beloved leader, and twenty-seven other Christians, were not going to be denied.

After first meeting heavy resistance from PLO fighters, and subduing them, the Phalanges then opened fire on civilians in the camps, massacring Palestinians and Shiite Arabs alike. Eight hundred civilians were killed, and General Sharon did not tell Menachem of the tragedy. Strangely, Begin heard the news on BBC radio – the same way he had learned about the approaching *Altalena*. Menachem would be heavily criticized and demonized, even by his fellow Israelis. His comment that "Christians massacre Muslims and the goyim blame the Jews predictably; foreign media are blaming us," fell on deaf ears both within and without Israel. But our hero would not blame Sharon. He would take full responsibility for what happened on himself, in spite of the turmoil surrounding the incident. The Knesset convened the Kahan Commission to determine with whom responsibility for the massacre lay.

After four months of deliberations, the commission determined that Ariel Sharon, more than the others, bore "special responsibility" for what had happened. Menachem tried to protect his friend Sharon, to no avail. Begin, frail and weakened by another stroke, accepted Sharon's resignation as defense minister. Another blow came when, while he was away visiting Los Angeles for a Jewish Federation meeting, he was informed that his ill wife, Aliza, had passed away. Our hero was now very depressed and lonely; he had lost his family in the war, and now the one positive from that period – the love of his life – was gone.

In retrospect, a 1982 letter to Senator Alan Cranston of Rhode Island reflected Begin's true belief regarding what had happened in Lebanon.

> The first horrific truth is that Arabs murdered Arabs. The second truth is that Israeli soldiers stopped the carnage. And the third truth is that if the current libelous campaign against Israel should go on without a reaction

of outrage from decent men – then within a matter of weeks or months everyone everywhere will have gotten the impression that it was an Israeli military unit which perpetrated the horrible killings.

Menachem never stopped believing that invading Lebanon was a war of necessity, a war of self-preservation. In spite of everything, Israel was the first country to confront terrorism at its core. It would not, could not, allow the PLO to attack northern Israel from southern Lebanon and tear their country apart. Israel, with Menachem Begin leading it, had protected itself and the Jewish people, regardless of the ensuing criticisms. The Western world – and the United States – would suffer the effects of terrorism in later years, with the 9/11 attacks as just one example.

Menachem was now alone, and due to his ongoing health maladies and hospitalizations he decided to resign as prime minister in August 1983 at the age of seventy. He told his colleagues, "I cannot go on any longer," and handed the government over to Yitzhak Shamir, former leader of the Lechi resistance movement.

His last years were spent living in an apartment overlooking the Jerusalem forest, mostly in seclusion. Finally, in March 1992, our hero suffered a severe heart attack in his apartment and fought hard to stay alive for six days. He finally succumbed at 3:30 a.m. on March 9, and a rabbi was summoned to say Kaddish for his soul.

He was buried in the Mount of Olives Jewish Cemetery in Jerusalem, where he had wanted to be interred, next to his beloved Aliza and nearby the graves of Meir Feinstein, of the Irgun, and Moshe Barazani, of the Lechi heroes, two who committed suicide while waiting in jail to be hanged by the British. Begin was voted the fourth-greatest Israeli of all time in a 2005 poll by the Israeli news website Ynet.

Our hero will be remembered for his love and respect for Jewish tradition, a love and respect that was returned in great measure by the Israeli people. Israel's have-nots – including Jews from Arab lands,

Ethiopia, etc. – had a warm feeling for Orthodox Judaism, which our hero enthusiastically embraced. Menachem was also a catalyst who paved the way for the yielding of the cultural elite (the Labor Party) to religious right-wing nationalism.

Menachem Begin was a decent, humane, and sensitive man who overcame tremendous obstacles to lead his people. His courage, morality, and belief in the redemption of the Jewish people from the Holocaust and antisemitism permeated his life. He was a true hero, whose total selfless devotion to his people, the Jewish people, overrode everything. His memory will live on in the annals of Jewish history as one of the truly great leaders.

Conclusion
||||||||||||||||||||||||||||

What is the definition of a hero? More specifically, what does it mean to be a Jewish hero? Yes, a hero is someone who exhibits tremendous courage and overcomes obstacles that the average person – a "mere mortal" – cannot or will not undertake. What other things make for a hero? Does our environment dictate the path we take? Or can anyone, rich or poor, become heroic?

In our stories of Jewish heroes down through the ages, we've seen amazing men and women, both rich and poor, achieve greatness through great deeds (Rabbi Akiva and his wife Rachel, Haym Salomon, and Menachem Begin to name a few). Did their Jewish backgrounds motivate them? Was it their belief in God that was their underlying motivation? Were they inspired to excel by the tradition that the world stands only upon study, work, and acts of loving-kindness (Ethics of the Fathers 1:2)? Why is it that since the inception of the Nobel Prize, 193 out of the 855 laureates have been Jewish? This is 22 percent of all Nobel recipients, yet Jews make up only 0.02 percent of the world's population!

Or did our Jewish heroes excel because of their strong belief in freedom (like Haym Salomon and Felix Zandman)? Or was it their vision that a Jewish state is necessary for the survival of the Jewish people (the Zionism of Theodor Herzl, Ze'ev Jabotinsky, David Ben-Gurion, Golda Meir, and Menachem Begin)?

All of our Jewish heroes, most from a very young age, understood their destinies and were driven to fulfill them – Haym Salomon and freedom from the British; Felix Zandman and surviving the Holocaust, then realizing tremendous success as a businessman and philanthropist; Golda Meir and her role in the creation of the state of Israel, along with Menachem Begin and David Ben-Gurion, not to mention Uriah P. Levy and the uncanny love for the sea he expressed in his youth. They ultimately achieved their goals and lived fascinating, challenging lives, but at what cost? How happy were they? What other similarities can be drawn between them? What lessons drawn from them?

Taking our eleven heroes' life stories and accomplishments, over thousands of years – or "down through the ages" – what qualities can we attribute to them in toto? Certainly most, if not all, exhibited unique intellectual abilities at a very early age. Haym Salomon, David Ben-Gurion, Ze'ev Jabotinsky, and Golda Meir all displayed notable intelligence as young children. Felix Zandman, at the age of fifteen, was able to learn advanced mathematics from his uncle (in a hole in the ground, no less). Haym Salomon knew and spoke six languages by the age of sixteen. So most of our heroes, if not all, were extremely bright and learned much at an early age.

What about leadership qualities? Were they born leaders? Yes, several were (Menachem Begin, Ze'ev Jabotinsky, and David Ben-Gurion; Golda Meir was already a youth leader at her school in Milwaukee at age eight), but some of our heroes didn't realize their callings until later in life (Rabbi Akiva, Queen Esther, Felix Zandman, Simon Wiesenthal). Their leadership qualities, their accomplishments, were developed in adulthood, not necessarily sooner. Why? For many, their leadership qualities were brought out when they were faced with life-threatening circumstances!

What about their Jewishness? Did our heroes hold close the knowledge that throughout history, tragedies have befallen the Jewish people time and again? Did they know of the destruction of the First and Second Temples in 432 BCE and 70 CE? Did they know of the First Crusade, in which tens of thousands of Jews were slaughtered, or of the expulsions of the Jews from England in 1290 and from Spain in 1492, as well as from many other countries and territories? Certainly these events overshadowed Jewish history, until World War II and the

Holocaust. We have seen that these Jewish heroes acknowledged and identified with their Jewish ancestry, and we can assume they were well aware of the history of their people.

Did all our heroes practice and embrace Judaism from an early age? Not necessarily – Rabbi Akiva, though Jewish by birth to an assimilated converted family, didn't embrace his religion until he met his wife, Rachel, in his twenties. Others, including David Ben-Gurion, Felix Zandman, Haym Salomon, and Menachem Begin, would maintain their deep belief in God and their Judaism their whole life through. So, some of our heroes were not the most religious adherents to Judaism and its practices. But in spite of that, they never denied their heritage and never lost sight of the plight of their fellow Jews – certainly not in Europe (where the majority of Jews lived at that time), before and during World War II.

Did our heroes believe in the ultimate power of God, that he was the one who allowed the Jewish people to finally have the Land of Israel back as their homeland? Our heroes certainly ranged in their levels of religious observance, but how can we discern belief in the Almighty in our heroes, or in any Jewish person? Is it religious observance? Going to services on Shabbat – the Day of Rest – and all holidays, all year through? Questions to ponder. I don't believe there is any clear answer.

What other qualities did our modern Zionist heroes display in their heroic journeys? For one, they all had the ability to communicate their stories effectively, to recite their message, whatever it might be, during their mission. Theodor Herzl, Ze'ev Jabotinsky, Menachem Begin, David Ben-Gurion, and Golda Meir all conveyed to the world that a Jewish state must be established, regardless of the odds against it, sooner rather than later. They were all great speakers and great writers; they got their messages across to all who would listen – the British, the Americans, the Germans, and their fellow Jews in Europe. Not everyone listened, but our heroes were never discouraged in their quest for a Zionist state.

What about antisemitism? How did it affect our heroes' lives and accomplishments? Golda Meir was harassed by Polish authorities as a "dirty Jew." Theodor Herzl saw the injustice visited upon Alfred Dreyfus by antisemitic mobs and the French "justice" system. Simon Wiesenthal lost eighty-nine members of his family to the Nazis' Final Solution. Felix Zandman saw his family taken away and massacred while still a young boy. All our heroes had their lives impacted by the scourge of antisemitism, their lives forever changed and molded by their experiences.

Were our eleven Jewish heroes influenced by their parents in their upbringing? Some definitely were, like David Ben-Gurion and Menachem Begin, who had strong father figures. Queen Esther adhered faithfully to the guidance of her cousin and adoptive father, Mordechai. Felix Zandman's role models were his grandmother, Tema Freydovicz, and his Uncle Sender, who both greatly influenced his early childhood and ambitions. Others, including Golda Meir, rebelled against their parents' control of their lives. Certainly Vladimir Jabotinsky, who lost his father at six, didn't have a strong paternal influence, though his mother did mark his bar mitzvah with a celebration when he was thirteen. David Ben-Gurion came from a religious home, but it was not Orthodox by any means. The early rallies he led as a young boy, advocating the establishment of a Jewish state, were rejected by the Orthodox, condemned as premature until the Messiah's appearance. Most assuredly Theodor Herzl, son of a well-to-do Hungarian family, was well educated by his parents and grew up in a comfortable environment in Budapest, Hungary. Uriah P. Levy, though born into a well-to-do family, went off on his own as a cabin boy at age ten! So our heroes had a "mixed bag" of parental guidance – not all had strong parental influences, and some rejected them outright, but they all became accomplished people regardless.

What about Zionism? How did our eleven amazing Jews feel about a Jewish homeland? There is no question that most, at an early age, felt the sting of antisemitism, and knew that living in a country hostile to Jews was not desirable. Even Haym Salomon, with his dream of freedom for the American colonies, suffered antisemitism before – and even after – his death. He would surely have been a sympathetic supporter of Zionism. Felix Zandman dreamed at an early age of a Jewish homeland, and later, as a very affluent business-man, he supported the State of Israel. He not only invented ingenious weaponry for the IDF, he built two successful factories for his company, Vishay Electronics, in Israel. Theodor Herzl, certainly, as well as Ze'ev Jabotinsky, the avowed Zionist Menachem Begin, the great David Ben-Gurion, and Golda Meir too – all were fervent Zionists, even as children. Many of our heroes knew that the Jewish state of Israel would be the one unifying force for the Jewish people; they rejected assimilation into unfriendly countries and pursued Zionism their entire lives.

Each of our eleven heroes was completely dedicated to his or her individual cause, whether that cause was freedom from the British (in the case of Haym Salomon), the establishment of a Jewish home-land (our Zionists), or the strong belief in Judaism and the worldwide spread of its influence and teachings (Rabbi Akiva). And we shouldn't neglect to mention Queen Esther, who, when confronted with the po-tential slaughter of her people, faced her king, and her husband, on her own terms. On the other hand, the need for survival, just to stay alive day to day, in an environment as close to a grave as one can get, was the challenge Felix Zandman met as a very young boy.

And family life? How did our eleven amazing people fare in this important aspect of their lives? Is it possible to devote one's life to a pas-sionate cause and still leave time to balance a true family commitment?

Tragically, some of our heroes had precious little time for their families. Certainly a cause like the creation of the State of Israel was all-consuming. Holidays and family events like birthdays and celebra-tions were all kept on the back burner. In Golda Meir's case, we have a prime example of children who hardly knew their mother. David Ben-Gurion lamented the passing of his wife for years because he had never been there for her. He even rejected the love of his life as a young man to pursue his passion – the Zionist dream. And how can we forget Rabbi Akiva, who, after marrying the beautiful, amazing Rachel, went away to study Torah for years, hardly seeing her? Certainly his sacrifice resonates down through the ages. He became a great rabbi, though at the cost of being an absentee husband and father. The brilliant Simon Wiesenthal, who could have been a successful architect, chose instead to seek justice for his fellow Jews, victims of the Nazi Holocaust. He lived a quiet, unassuming life, a bare existence, not caring for materialistic trappings. He truly sacrificed his life in his quest for justice.

So yes, our heroes paid heavy prices for their missions in life. They believed deeply in their purpose – and were guided by a strong belief in their goals as Jews. They overcame great obstacles and challenges, even though doing so meant paying a heavy price. In the end, though, each of our heroes had an enduring impact on all of our lives.

Our heroes' lives pose questions for us to ponder: Would George Washington have won at Yorktown without Haym Salomon? Would the Jews of Queen Esther's era have survived without her bravery? Would the world have advanced as far, as quickly, without the pioneering Israeli efforts in medicine and the miniaturization of electronic equipment (used in planes and military hardware, cell phones and communications technology) thanks to Felix Zandman?

Certainly, the State of Israel was founded in 1948 through the dedication and hard work of heroes such as Theodor Herzl, Ze'ev Jabotinsky, Menachem Begin, Golda Meir, and David Ben-Gurion. Israel today has achieved much of the dream they aspired to, and more. The country established to be a "light unto the nations" has achieved so much of that great goal.

Here is the briefest list of some of these achievements.

- Israel leads the world in impenetrable airline flight security.[33]

- Israel has more start-ups per capita than any other country in the world, and with 3,500 startups, more

---

33 Oren Liebermann, "In Airport Security, Many Say Ben Gurion in Israel Is the Safest," CNN, May 28, 2016, https://edition.cnn.com/travel/article/ben-gurion-worlds-safest-airport-tel-aviv/index.html.

than 3,000 in high-tech, is surpassed in real numbers only by the United States.[34]

- Israel leads the world in research and development, according to the 2018 Bloomberg Innovation Index.[35]

- The navigation app Waze was developed in Israel and sold to Google for over $1 billion.[36]

- The Microsoft Windows operating system was largely developed at Microsoft Israel, which continues to have a major role in the development of Microsoft technologies.[37]

- Voice mail and instant messaging were developed in Israel.[38]

- Drip irrigation was invented in Israel.[39]

---

34 "Did You Know: ISRAEL21c Brings Together Some of the Biggest Achievements That Have Come out of Israel," Israel21C, https://www.israel21c.org/israel-facts/technology/. See also Sam Shead, "The 25 Coolest Tech Companies in Israel," *Business Insider UK*, May 25, 2017, http://uk.businessinsider.com/coolest-tech-startups-in-israel-2017-5/#25-zebra-medical-diagnostics-company-1.

35 Michelle Jamrisko and Wei Lu, "The U.S. Drops Out of the Top 10 in Innovation Ranking," *Bloomberg Technology*, January 23, 2018, https://www.bloomberg.com/news/articles/2018-01-22/south-korea-tops-global-innovation-ranking-again-as-u-s-falls.

36 Julie Bort, "Waze Cofounder Tells Us How His Company's $1 Billion Sale to Google Really Went Down," *Business Insider*, August 13, 2015, http://www.businessinsider.com/how-google-bought-waze-the-inside-story-2015-8.

37 David Shamah, "Microsoft's Top New Tech, and Its Israel Connection, on Display at Think Next," April 23, 2012, https://www.timesofisrael.com/microsofts-top-new-tech-and-its-israel-connection-on-display-at-think-next/.

38 Heather McLean, "How Modern Life Is Made in Israel," *Telegraph*, June 16, 2007, http://www.telegraph.co.uk/technology/3353640/How-modern-life-is-made-in-Israel.html.

39 David Shamah, "What Israeli Drips Did for the World," *Times of Israel*, August 20 2013, https://www.timesofisrael.com/what-israeli-drips-did-for-the-world/.

- Israel is the country with the most museums per capita in the world.[40]

- The rocket-intercepting air defense system Iron Dome, which has stopped more than 1500 terrorist-fired rockets since its initial deployment in 2011, was developed by Rafael Advanced Defense Systems in Israel.[41]

In computers, cell phones, medicine, security, nanotechnology, health care, education, venture capital companies, military technology, and immigration, Israel is among the world's elite countries. The Jewish state is about tradition, history, and education, and has in fact become a "light unto the nations."

That the Jewish homeland is a free and open democracy would be a great source of satisfaction for all who endured antisemitism throughout the Jewish people's history in exile. Our eleven heroes would be proud of Israel and Jews around the world today – very, very proud indeed. We are indebted to our amazing heroes for all time, for all they have done to reshape our history, to continue the traditions of Jews, and to believe in our Jewish people and to make a positive difference for all of humanity.

---

40 Netta Ahituv, "10 of Israel's Best Museums," CNN, July 12, 2017, https://edition.cnn.com/travel/article/best-israel-museums/index.html.
41 Globes, "Report: US Eyes Purchase of Israel's Iron Dome to Defend European Bases," *Jerusalem Post*, September 10, 2017, http://www.jpost.com/Israel-News/Report-US-eyes-purchase-of-Israels-Iron-Dome-to-defend-European-bases-504699.

Afterword
||||||||||||||||||||||

My father, David Richard Goldberg, may be the last amazing Jewish hero covered in this book, but he was and will always be the first and most important Jewish hero in my book. I was fortunate enough to be one of many people who helped him compile this book. I feel incredibly blessed to have gone through this journey with him, before he passed away on October 23, 2016.

My father poured his heart and soul into making this book a reality. He spent countless days in the library researching the heroes, browsing the internet, and emailing, calling, and writing to many people around the world who helped him. During the writing of this book, I experienced yet another amazing side of him. To me, my father was always an incredible dad and leader of our family. He provided all the love, friendship, support, and guidance any son could ever hope for. What I did not know was how passionate he was to learn about the struggles that Jews have always faced and how important he thought it was to share Jewish values with others.

In fact, I know that in writing this book, his personal goal was to help educate Jews and non-Jews alike about all the challenges that the Jewish people have encountered in order to advance the cause of Zionism, form a Jewish state, and finally have the Jews stand on their own despite constant oppression from past civilizations, religions, and people. He was especially excited about the prospect of enlightening the younger generation, because they might not know what their ancestors fought for, what it really means to be a Jew, and how special it is to finally have our very own Jewish state.

I hope that you learned something from my dad's research, but I want to take a brief moment to tell you a little bit more about this great man and share with you why he is the most amazing Jewish hero I have personally ever known.

Throughout my own lifetime I witnessed his growth as a father, a friend, a businessman, and a Jew. The example he set to me was incomparable.

It is my personal belief that we are meant to use our time here on earth to grow, to become more giving, more selfless, and more "God-like" in nature. A newborn's first instinct after birth is to receive, rather than to give, and it takes a lifetime of learning and effort to become a great person. We must overcome many challenges through the journey of life. My father of course faced the same challenges.

Many years ago, he admitted to me that he was not perfect, and that even though he was my father and much older than me, he too had personal challenges that lingered. From our conversations together, I surmised that my dad felt deprived of love and support as a child. Growing up, his mother was disconnected from him, and his father was quite often absent. He simply did not get the love and support that many children do, and had emotional scars from his childhood that he carried deeply inside throughout his lifetime.

Instead of letting these emotional scars ruin his life, he chose to spend his lifetime overcoming his personal challenges. He chose to become someone with a giving nature rather than someone who was content to receive from others. He continued to grow personally and saw success in every facet of his personal, spiritual, and professional life. Anyone who met him instantly respected him as the perfect father figure, the perfect role model, and the perfect friend, and their admiration only grew the more they got to know him.

He gave his family everything he could, including unwavering love, friendship, guidance, loans to start businesses, a business partner to both sons and his son-in-law, relationship advice, and so on. He decided to give his family everything that he did not get as a child. Looking back now, this is easily the greatest quality I admired in him. He continued to grow, he continued to give all of himself and had success in every facet of his life both personally and professionally despite his difficult upbringing.

My father loved reading and writing. He wrote and published two books, one about his visit to Israel, titled *Our Trip to Israel: Memories of a Lifetime*, and the one that you are holding in your hands.

My father helped plant the seed for two successful businesses for all three of his children, and helped to grow them hands-on; my father was known as one of the most honest and trustworthy businessmen by all of his many clients and associates; my father had a lifelong love of boating and saved up for a cruising catamaran, which he sailed home across the ocean; my father fulfilled his lifelong dream of owning a vacation home in the mountains for our family to enjoy together; my father helped guide all of his children to successful marriages with beautiful families; my father adored my mother and tried to give her everything and anything she desired; my father led the alumni for his college; he was an ambassador to the American Friends of Magen David Adom (Israel's national first aid society), an avid supporter of the growth of his Chabad house and of his cherished rabbi Hershy Bronstein, and the list goes on and on. My father, quite simply, tried to help everyone he encountered as much as he could in every single aspect of their lives.

But the most important thing that my father did for us was not in business or leisure or the material comfort he provided, but in being the patriarch to our incredible family. Even up until the week before he passed away, he would continue to implore us to stay together no matter what obstacles we might face as a family. He taught us to respect one another, to love one another, to help one another, to always stay connected to Judaism, to communicate with one another, to laugh, to always have fun, and to embrace the gift that we all shared in simply having each other. He would almost never say no to any of us when we needed him (the only time he would was when he was teaching us an important life lesson). He was the biggest giver of love, advice, and support that anyone could ever imagine.

Family meant everything to my father, and he dedicated his life to helping make ours the best it could be. If I had a nickel for every time someone said to me how lucky we are to have such a close family, I would have retired many years ago. That was not a coincidence; it was through my father's commitment to leading our family through every important area of our personal lives and being the type of leader that you only see in movies.

So, I often asked myself, why did the last five months of his life unfold suddenly the way it did? I believe that my father overcame his personal challenges by continuing to grow and better himself throughout his lifetime, and that he accomplished everything possible that he or any man could hope for in a lifetime. It is my personal belief that his time here with us was complete. I also believe that the last five months between his birthday in May and Simchat Torah in October were a gift for those he cherished the most, his family. In this time we were lucky enough to be able to celebrate his life with him, to care for him as he had tirelessly cared for us, and to become even closer to him, day by day, before he moved on to a higher place.

My father died on the eve of Simchat Torah, when the Jewish people complete the Torah reading cycle and start anew again. My father also completed all he could on this earth and is starting anew again.

Although it is impossibly hard to not have my father here with me anymore, I know that besides leading a very successful and incredibly close family, this book was unquestionably his proudest achievement in life. So, however hard it may be for me to write these words down and help to complete this book, I know that somewhere up above he is beaming with delight at seeing his research and his passion for his people finally shared with the world. I hope you have gained something from it. I know that each person he touches with his words in this book will bring his spirit great joy.

Zachary Goldberg

November 2017

Resources
||||||||||||||||||||||

Rabbi Akiva

Lehmann, Marcus. Akiva: *The Story of Rabbi Akiva and His Times*. Nanuet, NY: Feldheim, 2003.

Queen Esther

Mindel, Nissan. "The Plot That Failed" and "Mordechai and Esther." In *The Complete Story of Purim*. New York: Kehot Publication Society, 1992.

Scheinberg, Chaim Pinchas. "A Lesson from Queen Esther." In *Heart to Heart Talks: Lectures to Women*. New York: ArtScroll/Mesorah, 2000.

Telushkin, Joseph. "Esther." In *Biblical Literacy: The Most Important People, Events, and Ideas of the Hebrew Bible*. New York: William Morrow, 1997.

Haym Salomon

Knight, Vick, Jr. *Send for Haym Salomon!* Alhambra, CA: Haym Salomon Foundation/Borden Publishing Co., 1976.

Moran, Donald S. "Haym Salomon, the Revolution's Indispensable Financial Genius." *Liberty Tree and Valley Compatriot Newsletter* (Los Angeles), October 1994.

Peters, Madison Clinton. *Haym Salomon: The Financier of the Revolution*. Stockton, CA: University of the Pacific, 2005.

URIAH P. LEVY

"Uriah Phillips Levy." In *Thomas Jefferson Encyclopedia,* Thomas Jefferson's Monticello. https://www.monticello.org/site/house-and-gardens/uriah-phillips-levy.

Stone, Kurt F. *The Jews of Capitol Hill: A Compendium of Jewish Congressional Members.* New York: Scarecrow Press, 2010.

FELIX ZANDMAN

Zandman, Felix, with David Chanoff. *Never the Last Journey.* New York: Schocken, 1995.

SIMON WIESENTHAl

"Simon Wiesenthal." Jewish Virtual Library. http://www.jewishvirtuallibrary.org/simon-wiesenthal.

Wechsberg, Joseph, ed. *The Murderers Among Us: The Wiesenthal Memoirs.* New York: McGraw-Hill, 1967.

THEODOR HERZL

Greenfeld, Howard. *A Promise Fulfilled: Theodor Herzl, Chaim Weizmann, David Ben-Gurion, and the Creation of the State of Israel.* New York: Greenwillow Books, 2005.

"Israel – 100 Years since Herzl's Death." *Jerusalem Report,* July 12, 2004.

Sharansky, Natan. *The Political Legacy of Theodor Herzl.* Jerusalem: Shalem Press, 2005.

"Theodor (Binyamin Ze'ev) Herzl." Jewish Virtual Library. http://www.jewishvirtuallibrary.org/theodor-binyamin-ze-rsquo-ev-herzl.

Vladimir (Ze'ev) Jabotinsky

Halkin, Hillel. *Jabotinsky: A Life*. New Haven, CT: Yale University Press, 2014.

David Ben-Gurion

Auerbach, Jerold S. *Brothers at War: Israel and the Tragedy of the Altalena*. New Orleans: Quid Pro Books, 2011.

Greenfeld, Howard. *A Promise Fulfilled: Theodor Herzl, Chaim Weizmann, David Ben-Gurion, and the Creation of the State of Israel*. New York: Greenwillow Books, 2005.

Kurzman, Dan. *Ben-Gurion: Prophet of Fire*. New York: Simon and Schuster, 1983.

Golda Meir

Burkett, Elinor. *Golda*. New York: HarperCollins, 2009.

Pogrebin, Letty Cottin. "Golda Meir." In *Jewish Women: A Comprehensive Historical Encyclopedia*, edited by Paula Hyman and Dalia Ofer. Jewish Women's Archives and Shalvi Publishing, 2006. https://jwa.org/encyclopedia/article/Meir-Golda.

Shenker, Israel. "Golda Meir: Peace and Arab Acceptance Were Goals of Her Five Years as Premier." *New York Times*, December 9, 1978. http://www.nytimes.com/learning/general/onthisday/bday/0503.html.

Menachem Begin

Feron, James. "Menachem Begin, Guerrilla Leader Who Became Peacemaker." *New York Times*, March 9, 1992. http://www.nytimes.com/1992/03/09/world/menachem-begin-guerrilla-leader-who-became-peacemaker.html?pagewanted=all.

Gordis, Daniel. *Menachem Begin: The Battle for Israel's Soul*. New York: Schocken, 2014.